SWEET

SPICY

SWEET SAVORY SPICY

EXCITING STREET MARKET FOOD
from Thailand, Cambodia, Malaysia and More

SARAH TIONG

MasterChef Australia finalist and owner
of Pork Party, a pop-up market stall

PAGE STREET
PUBLISHING CO.

PAGE STREET
PUBLISHING CO.

First published in 2020 by

Page Street Publishing Co.

27 Congress Street, Suite 105

Salem, MA 01970

www.pagestreetpublishing.com

Distributed by Macmillan, sales in Canada by The Canadian Manda Group.

24 23 22 21   5

ISBN-13: 978-1-64567-046-9

ISBN-10: 1-64567-046-5

Library of Congress Control Number: 2019951532

Cover and book design by Meg Baskis for Page Street Publishing Co.

Photography by Ben Cole

Printed and bound in China

DEDICATION

For my mother, brother and Aunty Annie, whose love and support have carried me so far. Thank you for teaching me resilience and gratitude and for sharing your love of food and family.

For Emilie and Jasmine, whose appetites for life and deliciousness have brought me undeniable happiness. Thank you for showing me true friendship.

CONTENTS

Sarah Tiong, you had me at Sweet, let alone Savory and Spicy!

This is the holy trinity of so many of the world's greatest dishes—dishes that have always inspired me to travel down seldom-trod roads, hunting for culinary unicorns. In the pages that follow, you'll find those culinary unicorns.

Street food always gets my attention, for it's my belief that the soul of a country's cuisine resides on the streets and in the stalls of ramshackle markets rather than in the starched linen of that country's fine-dining restaurants. There is nobility and ample tradition in these humble dishes.

On the street, flavors must roar and bellow to be heard above the honking of horns and the squeal of breaks. Everything is broader, prouder and a whole heap less fussy when you are perched on a tiny blue plastic chair in a Hanoi gutter, fighting the crowds for a rickety table in a sweating Bangkok night market or eating soy-sticky mee as dark as the night while the sweat-glazed faces of your dining companions jump in and out of shadows with the flaring of the woks.

Reading this book, you'll immediately know that these are the places where Sarah's heart must have roamed, whether as a child or as a hardworking corporate lawyer. Through hard work and a passion to explore flavor, she now finds herself "there"—living in these pages among the food she grew up with and the recipes she loves.

And it's here, at these stalls, carts and holes-in-the-wall across Asia, that every day at lunch and dinner (and all the hours in between), the locals vote with their wallets and their mouths on who makes what best. For us, however, Sarah has taken that heavy responsibility out of our hands and placed it firmly on to her shoulders, whether she's offering you her take on Malaysian Flatbread (page 69), Drunken Clams (page 61) or Vietnamese Grilled Pork Skewers (page 40).

She's also there, standing at your shoulder as you drool over her Khmer Beef Curry (page 107) or as your tongue and imagination play with the way the flavors of coconut and turmeric bounce against each other in the marinade for her version of Malaysian Barbecued Chicken with Coconut and Turmeric (page 19).

And when you cook these dishes, you'll hear her voice in the helpful advice laced through these recipes. Sarah guides you to create your own versions of many of the best street food dishes of Asia, whether you are re-creating a previous culinary adventure of your own or discovering for the first time the joys of these street food classics from Vietnam, Malaysia, Thailand and beyond.

Sarah is the perfect guide to these clogged and hungry streets, alleys and bustling market aisles, for she is a woman who loves to eat as much as she loves to cook. And boy, can she cook. When the inevitable question of, "Who's the best cook never to win *MasterChef Australia*?" comes up in interviews, my mind immediately flies to that tea plantation in the shadow of Mt. Fuji, where Sarah put her unique spin on the Singaporean classic of *bah kut teh* that brought tears to my eyes. I didn't well up because the dish was so darned delicious but because I felt that Sarah had liberated the spirit of this famous hawker pork rib broth and sent it wheeling and soaring to new heights. Only very special dishes from very special cooks do that.

Enough! I've got to go, because I've got a hot date with the Grilled Mussels with Lime and Pepper Sauce on page 44. I hope it will send my soul soaring to similar heights!

—*MATT PRESTON,* author of *More* and six other bestselling cookbooks and former cohost and judge on *MasterChef Australia*

My mother always described me as a "good eater," unfussy and fearless in the face of all things weird and delicious. It wasn't a very difficult title to hold growing up in a large, passionate family who loved to cook and eat. My mother migrated from a tiny village in Sibu, Sarawak, Malaysia, to the big city of Sydney, Australia, in the 1970s at the tender age of seventeen with nothing but a shabby suitcase, a skinny fiancé and a perfect perm. She had no cooking experience. Relying only on her memory, yearning for Malaysian street food and the simple home cooking of her childhood, Mum endeavored to re-create the flavors of Malaysia as best as she could. Those are the flavors she passed down to me.

Authentic Southeast Asian food is street food. The street carts, hawker centers and open-air food courts in Southeast Asia are where you find real people cooking real food. They've been cooking the same food for generations, perfecting techniques and mastering flavors. Street food is powerful—it connects people, creates identity and impacts generations to come. I inherited Mum's vivaciousness and appetite for the delicious, unique food that she experienced growing up around hawker centers, kopitiams (coffee shops) and street carts. I am extremely lucky to have grown up in a family that finds passion and joy in the pursuit of exquisite food.

Family vacations and visits to Southeast Asia were how my love of street food was nurtured. The night markets were a culinary wonderland and my favorite part of the holidays. The most nostalgic, powerful, reactive memories I have are triggered by the smell of charcoal barbecues, *belachan* (shrimp paste) and coconut. Some of my happiest food memories are of eating tender satay off a stick or slurping down bowls of noodles from roadside stalls in Malaysia and Singapore. My travels to Cambodia, Thailand and beyond in my teen and early adult years sparked a passion and curiosity for street food. The heat and noise of the markets, hawker centers and food carts of Southeast Asia create the most exciting energy. The recipes I have written in this book all aim to bring that energy to your home.

I'm a lawyer by trade. I've spent years in giant financial services and insurance firms. While I love being a lawyer, it pales in comparison to the passion and thrill I feel when I am cooking for others. It seemed only logical for me to apply to compete on *MasterChef Australia* in 2017 after years of being a fan of the show. The *MasterChef* experience was a complete whirlwind of adrenaline, discovery and endurance. I thrived. I was the top-six finalist of my year. Thousands of people had applied to the show, and I cooked my heart out, showcasing Southeast Asian cuisine and inspiration. It was a pivotal moment in my life. As soon as I left *MasterChef*, I started developing recipes for the Australian pork industry, judging national barbecue competitions, holding master classes with some of the biggest brands and shopping centers in Australia and started my own street food pop-up stall, Pork Party.

(continued)

Pork Party's philosophy is simple: Create and produce pork-based street food with Southeast Asian flavors. I've been fortunate to have immense success with Pork Party. The market stall continues to this day at special events around Sydney, Australia.

In 2020, *MasterChef Australia* came calling and selected me to be a returning contestant for season twelve. It stoked the fire within me, and I just could not pass on the opportunity. It's not every day you get a second serving of such success! I am so grateful for how well I have been received and how supported I feel by fans of the show. My career continues to expand in the food industry. I'm a private chef, food-event organizer, traveling cook and now an author. This book is a collection of my memories and inspiration from my firsthand experiences with the richness of Southeast Asia's culture, its complex and tangled history and the beauty of its diversity. This is my way of sharing my decades of expertise with Southeast Asian food with you and showing you how easy it is to create exciting, impressive flavors at home.

There is a marvelous intensity and boldness of flavor in Southeast Asian food that is unique to that part of the world. There are sights, sounds and textures that make your heart race and mouth water. Just imagine the sensual smokiness of noodles, fried over wok burners that look and sound like flaming rocket jets. Or the sweet, sticky temptations of treats that seem to be so satisfyingly crispy yet wonderfully chewy at the same time. I hope this book whets your appetite, makes you curious and helps you and your loved ones fall in love with the remarkable deliciousness of Southeast Asian flavors.

ON THE BARBECUE

Barbecuing is an integral part of Southeast Asian culture. There are alleyways and street blocks dedicated to impressive spreads of seafood and meats spiced and slathered in sauce, marinated in turmeric and coconut and crisping up on beds of charcoal. Night markets are lined with rows of charred skewered meat glistening with sticky, oily glazes. Wherever you are in Southeast Asia, the rising smoke, glowing coals and enticing aromas of spices and grilled meats are seductive. This chapter captures how my love affair with cooking outdoors and cooking with fire started. These recipes are the ones that have enticed me the most throughout my life. The smoky, juicy flair of my Malaysian Barbecued Chicken with Coconut and Turmeric (page 19), the spicy, crispy bits of Malaysian Grilled Whole Fish with Sambal (page 35) and the sticky, jammy sweetness of Grilled Corn with Spicy Tamarind Butter (page 31) represent delicious moments of togetherness with loved ones, sharing dishes and eating with your hands.

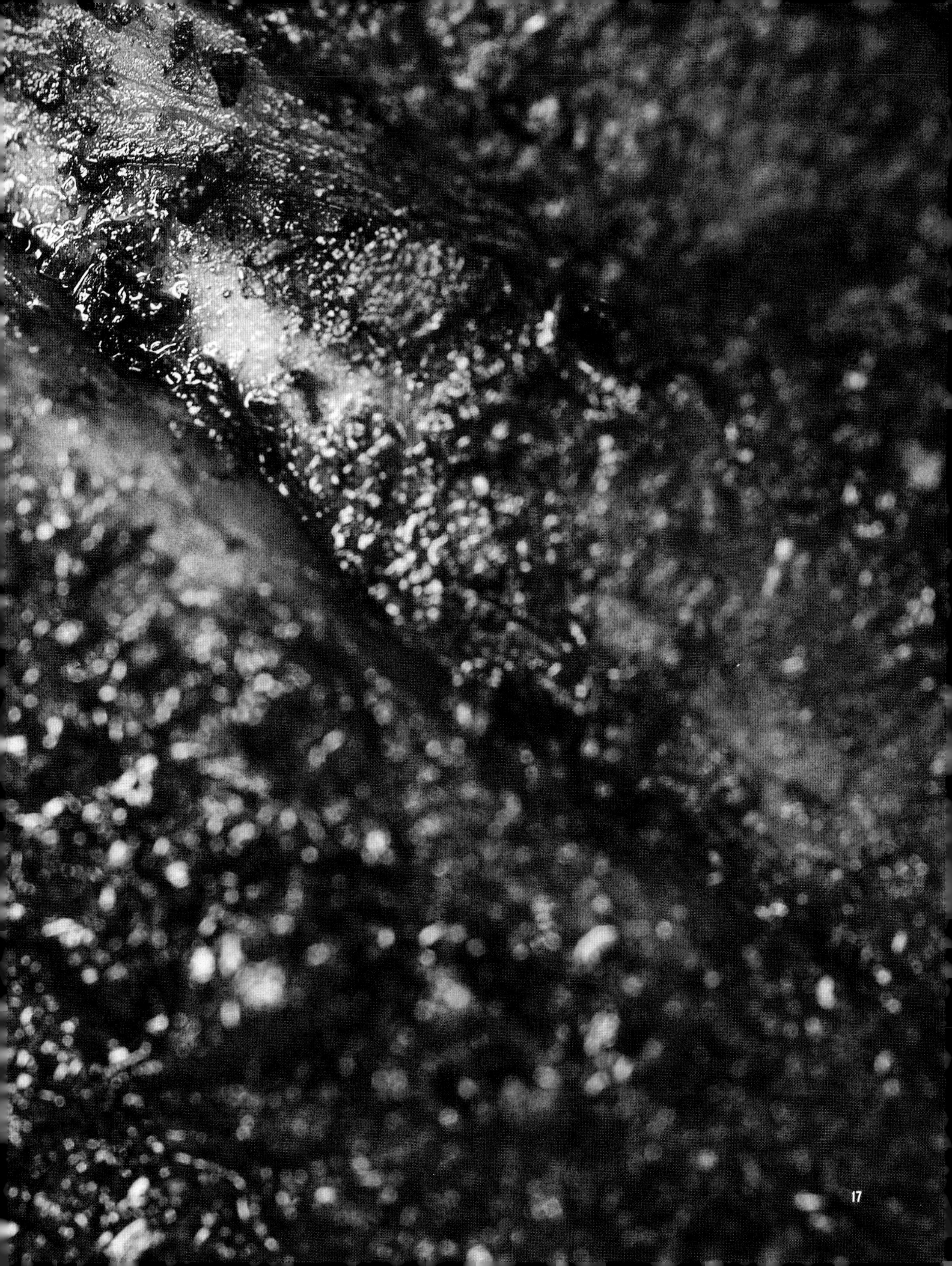

MALAYSIAN BARBECUED CHICKEN WITH COCONUT AND TURMERIC

(AYAM PERCIK)

This is one of the juiciest, most delicious chicken recipes you can cook. The trick is to keep gently basting the chicken with the marinade. The chicken becomes a beautiful golden color with little spots of charring from the charcoal. The fragrance of coconut, turmeric and lemongrass paired with the mouthwatering aroma of smoky grilled chicken is one of the most exciting combinations possible. For best results, cook this recipe over a charcoal grill. Alternatively, this chicken can be roasted in the oven at 375°F (191°C) for 50 minutes and rested for 15 minutes.

MAKES 1 WHOLE CHICKEN

MARINADE

5 cloves garlic, minced or grated

3 large red Asian shallots, finely chopped

1 (1½-inch [4-cm]) piece fresh ginger, unpeeled

3 medium stalks lemongrass (white parts only), thinly sliced

6 toasted whole candlenuts or macadamia nuts

2 tbsp (18 g) five-spice powder

1 tbsp (9 g) ground coriander

2 tsp (6 g) ground turmeric

1 tsp ground black pepper

1 tsp hot chili powder

2½ tsp (13 g) salt

1 tbsp (12 g) sugar

1 cup (240 ml) full-fat coconut milk

Juice of 1 medium lime

½ cup (120 ml) rice bran, canola or grapeseed oil

CHICKEN

1 (3⅓- to 4-lb [1.5- to 1.8-kg]) whole chicken, butterflied

½ cup (120 ml) full-fat coconut milk

¼ cup (60 ml) neutral-flavored (rice bran, canola or grapeseed) oil

Lime wedges, as needed

To make the marinade, combine the garlic, shallots, ginger, lemongrass, candlenuts, five-spice powder, coriander, turmeric, black pepper, chili powder, salt, sugar, coconut milk, lime juice and oil in a blender. Blend until the ingredients are smooth. Reserve one-third of the marinade and set it aside.

To make the chicken, place the whole chicken in a large zip-top bag. Rub the remaining two-thirds of marinade into the chicken, ensuring the entire surface is coated. Place the zip-top bag in a large bowl or on a large baking sheet and transfer it to the refrigerator to marinate overnight (or for up to 2 days).

In a large bowl, mix together the reserved marinade, coconut milk and oil. Stir thoroughly to combine. This is the basting marinade.

Remove the chicken from the refrigerator 30 minutes before you want to grill it.

Preheat the grill to medium heat (350°F [177°C]). Place the chicken on the grill, breast side down. Grill the chicken for 8 to 10 minutes, then flip it and baste it with the basting marinade. Grill the chicken for another 20 to 30 minutes, flipping and basting it every 5 to 6 minutes, until the internal temperature reads 165°F (74°C) in the thickest part of the meat.

Let the chicken rest for 5 to 10 minutes before serving it with the lime wedges.

CAMBODIAN PORK CHOPS

One of the greatest street cart meals I ever had in Cambodia was this grilled pork chop right off the white-hot coals. It was served in a Styrofoam clamshell box and as soon as I opened the lid, I was hit with the distinct smell of pepper and lemongrass. These flavors worked perfectly with the steamed rice and pickled vegetables nestled next to the pork. Feel free to trade the pork for your preferred protein—this recipe works particularly well with beef and veal steaks.

SERVES 2

1 tbsp (9 g) black peppercorns

1 large star anise pod

2 medium stalks lemongrass (white parts only)

3 cloves garlic

4 tbsp (60 ml) rice bran, canola or grapeseed oil, plus more as needed

1½ tsp (8 g) salt

2 (1-inch [2.5-cm]-thick) bone-in pork chops (preferably rib chops, with the rind on or off)

SERVING SUGGESTIONS

Steamed rice or rice noodles, toasted peanuts and assorted pickles (radishes, carrots, cucumbers, chilies)

In a dry, small skillet over low heat, toast the peppercorns and star anise for 4 to 5 minutes, until they are dark and aromatic.

Using the back of a knife, a rolling pin or a pestle, bruise the stalks of lemongrass by crushing them. Thinly slice the bruised lemongrass. In a mortar and pestle, crush together the peppercorns, star anise, garlic and lemongrass to form a coarse paste. Add the oil and salt and mix everything together thoroughly. Alternatively, if you don't have a mortar and pestle, use a spice grinder to crush the spices. Mince the lemongrass and garlic and place them in a small bowl. Then add the spice mixture and stir in the oil and salt to create a paste.

Massage all of the pepper marinade into the pork chops. Transfer the pork chops to the refrigerator and allow them to marinate for at least 2 hours.

Remove the pork chops from the refrigerator about 30 minutes before you intend to cook them so they come closer to room temperature.

In the meantime, preheat the grill to medium-high heat (400 to 450°F [204 to 232°C]).

Drizzle a little oil over each of the pork chops. Lay them on the grill and cook them on one side for 4 to 5 minutes. Flip the pork chops and cook on the other side for 2 to 3 minutes, until the internal temperature reaches between 125 and 135°F (52 and 57°C) for medium-rare doneness. (Medium-rare pork will have some pink in the center of the chop; this is ideal for pork chops and will ensure juiciness.) Remove the pork chops from the grill and let them rest for 5 minutes.

Serve the pork chops with rice, toasted peanuts and assorted pickles. Pour the resting juices over the pork chops just prior to serving.

TIPS: The pork chops can be marinated the day before.

The pork chops will blacken while they cook. Don't worry about this; it's a mixture of sugars from the marinade and the black pepper. Lower the grill to medium heat (350°F [177°C]) if you feel the chops are blackening too fast.

The pork chops can be cooked for 4 to 5 minutes per side in a griddle pan over medium-high heat on the stove. Rest them for 5 minutes once they are cooked.

This marinade works with minute steaks too, which means you can skip the 2-hour marinating time. Just simply rub pork, veal or beef minute steaks with the marinade and cook them on the grill for just under 1 minute on each side.

VIETNAMESE GRILLED BEEF WRAPPED IN BETEL LEAVES
(BÒ LÁ LOT)

Some of the most unique ingredients and flavors are found in Southeast Asia. Just like the people, the types of herbs and spices are wonderfully diverse. Betel leaves are a beautiful example of this diversity. I first came across these heart-shaped leaves in Vietnamese cuisine, followed by Indian cuisine, and I was surprised to learn just how differently the leaves were used in different cultures. My favorite application is in this Vietnamese recipe. Betel leaves don't have much of an aroma when raw—but when they are grilled, they release a perfume of sweet pepperiness with a hint of smoky vanilla and sage. Paired with tender beef and toasted peanuts, the flavor combination in this dish is warm and inviting.

YIELD: 12 ROLLS

8 oz (224 g) beef, sliced into ½-inch (13-mm)-wide strips (see Tip)

2 medium stalks lemongrass (white parts only), finely chopped

1 large red Asian shallot, finely chopped

2 cloves garlic, finely chopped

1 tsp ground black pepper

1 tbsp (15 ml) oyster sauce

2 tsp (10 ml) fish sauce

2 tsp (10 ml) light soy sauce

1 tbsp (15 ml) rice bran, canola or grapeseed oil, plus more as needed

12 large fresh betel leaves

¼ cup (30 g) crushed roasted peanuts

FOR SERVING

Large lettuce leaves

Rice paper

Vietnamese mint leaves or regular mint leaves

Spring onions, sliced into 2-inch (5-cm)-long pieces

Fresh cilantro stems and leaves

Lime wedges

Vietnamese Spicy Dipping Sauce (Nuoc Cham) (page 127)

In a large bowl, combine the beef, lemongrass, shallot, garlic and pepper and mix them together thoroughly. Add the oyster sauce, fish sauce, soy sauce and oil. Mix the ingredients well and let the beef marinate for at least 30 minutes. (You can prepare the beef a day ahead of grilling.)

Lay a betel leaf with the flat, dull side facing upward, the tip facing toward you and the stalk facing away. Place 3 or 4 strips of beef horizontally on the lower half of the leaf. Roll the leaf up into a little parcel. Secure the leaf by threading the stalk through the leaf or using a toothpick. Repeat this process with the remaining betel leaves and beef.

If you have used toothpicks, you won't need to skewer the little parcels together. If you haven't used toothpicks, take a long skewer that has been soaked in water for at least 30 minutes and skewer 4 of the parcels together on one end, about 1 inch (2.5 cm) in from the edge of the leaf. Use a second skewer to go through the opposite end of the parcels, also about 1 inch (2.5 cm) in from the edge. This arrangement will help you make more controlled turns on the grill. Repeat this step for all the parcels.

Preheat the grill to medium-high heat (400 to 450°F [204 to 232°C]).

Brush each of the parcels lightly with some oil. Grill the parcels for 2 to 3 minutes per side, until the beef begins to cook through and the leaves become charred and crispy. Transfer the parcels to a plate, remove any toothpicks and scatter the peanuts over the top of the parcels.

Serve the wrapped beef with lettuce leaves or rice paper, mint, spring onions, cilantro, lime wedges and Vietnamese Spicy Dipping Sauce (Nuoc Cham).

TIP: Use a cut of beef like rump, topside or sirloin for this recipe.

GRILLED SAMBAL BUTTER PRAWNS

Buttery, savory, irresistible—this is an incredible barbecued prawn recipe that has been a family favorite forever. In Malaysia, this dish is usually saucier and sweeter than this version, as ketchup is typically added. Over the years, my family has adjusted the original recipe to this simple and savory version that is super quick to whip up at barbecues. The Sambal Belachan (a spicy shrimp paste sauce, page 120) adds a fragrant, spicy kick. The prawn meat is cooked gently and soaks up the flavored butter along with some of the smoky flavor from the grill. The shell becomes beautifully caramelized and charred while protecting the meat. This recipe would work well with lobster or crayfish too.

SERVES 10

9 oz (252 g) salted butter, softened

4 tbsp (60 g) Sambal Belachan (page 120) or store-bought sambal belachan

3 large red serrano chilies, seeds removed (optional) and finely chopped

3 cloves garlic, finely chopped

Salt, as needed

20 extra-large, shell-on fresh prawns

Lemon wedges, for serving

Preheat the grill to medium-high heat (400 to 450°F [204 to 232°C]). In a medium bowl, mix together the butter, Sambal Belachan, serrano chilies, garlic and a pinch of salt to create the sambal butter.

Using a serrated knife, carefully butterfly each prawn by cutting through the back of the prawn about three-quarters of the way through its body, leaving the belly intact. Cut right from the top of the head, near the eyes, all the way down to the tail. Remove the vein from the back of the prawn and open up the prawn wider by gently pushing each half of the prawn back so it butterflies open.

Using a spoon or spatula, spread a generous amount of the sambal butter into the center of each prawn.

Grill the prawns, shell side down, for 4 to 5 minutes, until the prawns become opaque and the butter has melted.

Alternatively, preheat the oven to broil. Line a large baking sheet with foil. Place the prawns on the prepared baking sheet and place the baking sheet on the top rack of the oven. Broil the prawns for 5 to 6 minutes, or until the flesh is completely opaque and there is some charring.

Serve the prawns with the lemon wedges.

JALAN ALOR GRILLED CHICKEN WINGS

Jalan Alor is one of the most famous streets in Kuala Lumpur, Malaysia, housing an amazing array of hawkers, food carts and restaurants. Everything crispy, sticky, sweet, savory, tangy, smoky and tender is available on Jalan Alor. One of the most delicious things to order from a famous restaurant at the end of the street called Wong Ah Wah are these dark, shiny chicken wings that are cooked on charcoal barbecues. They're marinated in aromatic spices and glazed with a bit of honey. The best thing about these wings is that they are not too sticky or sweet.

SERVES 3 TO 4

MARINADE

½ cup (120 ml) light soy sauce

¼ cup (60 ml) dark soy sauce

½ cup (120 ml) rice bran, canola or grapeseed oil

2 tbsp (30 ml) honey

2 tsp (4 g) ground black pepper

3 cloves garlic, finely grated

1 (1½-inch [4-cm]) piece fresh ginger, finely grated

3 large red Asian shallots, finely chopped

CHICKEN WINGS

10 whole chicken wings

SERVING SUGGESTION

Mum's "Everything" Sauce (page 115)

To make the marinade, combine the light soy sauce, dark soy sauce, oil, honey, black pepper, garlic, ginger and shallots in a large bowl. Reserve one-third of the mixture in a small bowl and refrigerate it.

To make the chicken wings, add the chicken wings to the remaining marinade in the large bowl. Toss them well to coat them. Transfer the bowl to the refrigerator and allow the chicken wings to marinate for at least 2 hours (or overnight).

Preheat the grill to medium-high heat (400 to 450°F [204 to 232°C]). Remove the chicken wings from the refrigerator 30 minutes before grilling. Toss the wings again to redistribute the marinade over them. Grill the chicken wings for 15 to 20 minutes, flipping and basting the wings with the reserved marinade every 1 to 2 minutes, until the wings are slightly charred and their internal temperature reaches 165°F (74°C).

Alternatively, preheat the oven to broil. Line a large baking sheet with foil. Place the chicken wings on the prepared baking sheet and place the baking sheet on the top rack of the oven. Broil the chicken wings for 8 to 9 minutes per side, until their internal temperature reaches 165°F (74°C).

Serve the chicken wings with Mum's "Everything" Sauce.

VIETNAMESE GRILLED PORK RIBS

The caramel-like sweetness of brown sugar, the pungency and saltiness of fish sauce and the zing of lime on these sticky, tender ribs transports me to warm evenings with my friends and family, sitting by the grill on the banks of the Mekong River. Barbecued ribs have the effect of bringing everyone together. There's something about eating with your hands and pulling the meat off the bones that puts a smile on everyone's face. The best thing about these ribs is that they've been marinated in grated onion. This tenderizes the meat and allows them to grill quickly.

SERVES 4

PORK RIBS

2 medium brown or yellow onions, grated

3 cloves garlic, grated

2 tbsp (18 g) five-spice powder

2 tsp (10 g) salt

2 tbsp (30 ml) rice bran, canola or grapeseed oil, plus more as needed

1 (2½-lb [1.1-kg]) rack baby back pork ribs

BASTING SAUCE

2 tbsp (18 g) brown sugar dissolved in 1 tbsp (15 ml) water

4 cloves garlic, grated

2 medium stalks lemongrass (white parts only), trimmed and finely chopped

1 tsp hot chili powder (optional)

1 tsp ground black pepper

Juice of 1 medium lime

Zest of 1 medium lime

½ tbsp (8 ml) light soy sauce

½ tbsp (8 ml) dark soy sauce

1 tbsp (15 ml) fish sauce

¼ cup (60 ml) rice bran, canola or grapeseed oil

To make the pork ribs, mix together the onions, garlic, five-spice powder, salt and oil in a large bowl. Add the pork ribs and stir to cover them with the marinade. Allow them to marinate for at least 2 hours at room temperature (or overnight in the refrigerator).

To make the basting sauce, combine the brown sugar, garlic, lemongrass, chili powder (if using), black pepper, lime juice, lime zest, light soy sauce, dark soy sauce, fish sauce and oil in a medium bowl.

Preheat the grill to medium-high heat (400 to 450°F [204 to 232°C]).

Brush the marinade from the ribs and rub a small amount of oil on both sides. Grill the ribs, meat side down, for 7 minutes. Flip the ribs and grill them for another 7 minutes, basting the meat side with the basting sauce, until the pork's internal temperature reaches 145°F (63°C).

Flip the ribs again and grill them for 7 minutes, basting the bone side.

Flip the ribs one final time and grill them for 7 minutes. Baste the ribs all over before removing them from the heat.

Let the ribs rest for 5 to 10 minutes before serving.

GRILLED CORN
WITH SPICY TAMARIND BUTTER

One of my greatest food memories with my family in Malaysia is coming across a street food cart parked in the middle of a neighborhood lane, steam rising and filling the air with the aroma of sweet corn. The corn cobs were plump, golden and slathered with Planta, the most iconic margarine brand of my childhood. This vegetarian recipe is an updated version that adds a bit of excitement to barbecues with the delicious tang of tamarind and a kick of heat.

When purchasing corn, you want plump kernels and bright-green, tight husks. The silk poking out of the top should be golden and a little damp or tacky. These are all signs of freshness—if the husk is yellowing and the silk is dry, the corn is old.

SERVES 4

4 ears corn, husk on

3½ oz (98 g) unsalted butter, softened

2 cloves garlic, grated or minced

2 tbsp (30 g) tamarind paste

2 tsp (6 g) hot chili powder

1½ tsp (8 g) salt

Finely chopped fresh cilantro, as needed

Bring a large pot of salted water to a boil over high heat. Add the corn and boil it for 3 minutes. Drain the corn and allow it to cool to room temperature.

In the meantime, mix together the butter, garlic, tamarind paste, chili powder and salt in a small bowl, stirring to combine.

Carefully peel back the husk of each ear of corn, keeping it attached, and remove the silk. Using a small spatula or brush, coat each ear of corn with the tamarind butter, dividing the butter evenly among the ears of corn. Fold the husks back over the buttered corn. You could prepare the corn, up to this step, 1 or 2 days before grilling.

Preheat the grill to medium heat (350°F [177°C]). Grill the corn for 5 to 6 minutes, turning the corn every minute, until the husks have charred. Alternatively, you can cook the corn under the broiler for the same time.

Serve the corn hot and sprinkled with the cilantro.

TIPS: If your corn does not have husks, you can wrap the buttered corn with aluminum foil for the same effect.

The tamarind butter works well with other grilled vegetables, like sweet potatoes, Brussels sprouts and eggplant.

BARBECUED SQUID

(SOTONG BAKAR)

In Malaysia and Thailand, I saw the most amazing array of seafood grilled over charcoal. Something that caught my eye immediately was the large whole grilled squid. The legs had been separated in order to clean the inside of the squid, but the body was kept whole. The crispy, deep gold char on the squid was seductive. Once the squid came off the grill, the cooks brushed it with a fragrant garlic oil. The dish was the perfect combination of saltiness, oiliness and tenderness. This is truly one of my favorite barbecue dishes.

SERVES 4

2 cloves garlic, thinly sliced

4 spring onions, thinly sliced

1 (1½-inch [4-cm]) piece fresh ginger, grated

½ cup (120 ml) rice bran, canola or grapeseed oil

2½ tsp (13 g) salt, divided

½ tsp ground star anise

½ tsp ground black pepper

1 (2-lb [900-g]) whole squid, cleaned

Preheat the grill to high heat (450 to 475°F [232 to 246°C]). In a small saucepan over medium heat, combine the garlic, spring onions, ginger, oil and 1 teaspoon of the salt. Cook this mixture for 10 to 15 minutes, until it is very fragrant and the garlic is a deep gold color. If the garlic starts to brown too quickly, remove the saucepan from the heat for 2 minutes and then place it over low heat.

In a small bowl, combine the remaining 1½ teaspoons (8 g) of salt, star anise and black pepper.

Pat the squid dry and season it liberally all over with the salt mixture. Brush some of the spring onion oil over the squid. Place the squid on the grill and cook it for 3 to 4 minutes on one side, or until the inside of the squid has become opaque and the outside is golden and lightly charred around the edges. Turn the squid over, baste it with the spring onion oil and cook it for an additional 3 to 4 minutes. (Larger squids may take longer to cook.) Reserve the rest of the spring onion oil.

Remove the squid from the grill and allow it to rest for 2 to 3 minutes before slicing it into bite-size pieces.

Arrange the sliced squid on a platter and top it generously with the spring onions and garlic from the oil and drizzle the remaining oil over the top. Serve the squid warm.

TIP: The resting juices and oil on the bottom of the platter are great to dip sticky rice or bread into.

MALAYSIAN GRILLED WHOLE FISH WITH SAMBAL

(IKAN BAKAR)

One of the most enticing experiences in Malaysia is walking by the roadside barbecue restaurants and seeing the incredible assortment of fish lining the grills. There are brilliant yellows from turmeric, reds and oranges from chili and spice powders and green ribbons of banana leaves. Then you dig into the succulent fish marinated in the most exciting sambal, and it feels like pure happiness. This recipe works with fillets and whole fish. Choose fish with firm flesh that doesn't flake apart too easily. Suitable options include snapper, black sea bass, mackerel or branzino.

SERVES 3 TO 4

MARINADE PASTE

6 large red serrano chilies, seeds removed (optional) and finely chopped

3 large red Asian shallots, roughly chopped

4 cloves garlic

2 tsp (10 g) toasted shrimp paste (belachan)

2 medium stalks lemongrass (white parts only), thinly sliced

1 tsp ground turmeric

1 to 2 tbsp (15 to 30 ml) water, as needed

FISH

6 tbsp (90 ml) rice bran, canola or grapeseed oil

3 tbsp (45 g) tamarind paste

1 tbsp (12 g) sugar

2 tsp (10 g) salt

1 (3-lb [1.4-kg]) fresh, whole, firm whitefish, cleaned

1 strip banana leaf, long and wide enough to wrap around the fish

Juice of 1 medium lime

To make the marinade, combine the chilies, shallots, garlic, shrimp paste, lemongrass and turmeric in a food processor and process until the ingredients are very fine. Add 1 to 2 tablespoons (15 to 30 ml) of water to the mixture and continue processing until the mixture becomes a paste.

To make the fish, heat the oil in a medium skillet or wok over medium-high heat. Carefully add the marinade paste and tamarind paste to the hot oil and fry the pastes for 5 to 6 minutes, stirring frequently, or until the oil splits from the pastes and rises to the top. Add the sugar and salt and stir-fry the mixture for 3 to 4 minutes to dissolve the sugar and salt. Remove the mixture from the heat and allow it to cool.

Once the marinade has cooled, rub it all over the fish and inside its cavity, ensuring all of its surfaces are covered. Allow the fish to marinate for at least 2 hours in the refrigerator.

Remove the fish from the refrigerator at least 30 minutes before you intend to grill it and allow it to come close to room temperature. (This helps ensure the fish won't stick to the barbecue.)

In the meantime, preheat the grill to medium-high heat (400 to 450°F [204 to 232°C]). Lightly grease the grill.

Place the fish on the banana leaf and wrap the leaf around the fish, securing it with a toothpick or skewer. Then place the fish onto the grill and cook it, undisturbed, for 6 to 8 minutes. Flip the fish and cook it for another 6 to 8 minutes. If the fish does not release from the grill when it is time to flip it, reduce the heat to low and try again in 1 or 2 minutes. The fish is done when the flesh has turned opaque and the fish releases from the grill.

Allow the fish to rest, wrapped, for 4 to 5 minutes before dressing with lime juice and serving.

TIP: **This recipe pairs perfectly with Grilled Sticky Rice with Dried Shrimp and Coconut (page 39) and Papaya Salad (page 54).**

GRILLED SPICY PINEAPPLE

Pineapples are like gems of joy in Southeast Asia. They're tropical, juicy, sweet and a little tart. They make your mouth water and pair perfectly with the smoky aroma of charcoal. This pineapple is great to add to your grilling repertoire—served with savory dishes or with ice cream for dessert, it is sure to be a crowd-pleaser. This recipe can be made vegetarian by omitting the fish sauce.

SERVES 8

4 large red serrano chilies, seeds removed (optional) and minced

1 (1½-inch [4-cm]) piece fresh ginger, grated

2 tsp (4 g) ground coriander

6 tbsp (90 ml) light soy sauce

1 tbsp (15 ml) fish sauce

Juice of 1 medium lime

3 tbsp (27 g) brown sugar

1 large pineapple, peeled and cut lengthwise into 8 long wedges

Zest of 1 lime

Thinly sliced fresh mint leaves

In a medium bowl, mix together the chilies, ginger, coriander, soy sauce, fish sauce, lime juice and brown sugar. Stir the mixture until the brown sugar dissolves.

Place the wedges of pineapple in a large baking dish or in a zip-top bag. Pour the marinade over the pineapple. Mix well and allow the pineapple to marinate for at least 30 minutes, stirring or shaking the pineapple occasionally.

In the meantime, preheat the grill to medium heat (350°F [177°C]).

Grill the pineapple for 3 to 4 minutes per side, until it is caramelized, softened and cooked through.

Place the pineapple on a platter and sprinkle it with the lime zest and mint leaves before serving.

TIP: **You can leave the seeds in the chilies for an extra spicy kick!**

GRILLED STICKY RICE WITH DRIED SHRIMP AND COCONUT

(PULUT PANGGANG)

Pulut panggang (grilled sticky rice wrapped in banana leaves) is an absolute must at all my family barbecues and a great little treat from street food carts in Malaysia. I fell in love with these gorgeous, smoky banana leaf parcels as a child. Once you peel away the charred banana leaves, you're greeted with glossy sticky rice with crispy golden edges, chewy insides and a sweet and savory filling. The combination of dried shrimp and coconut is irresistible. This recipe requires a bit of work, but the result is worth it. These sticky rice parcels can be eaten hot or cold and can be prepared a day before grilling.

MAKES 12 PARCELS

STICKY RICE

1½ cups (315 g) glutinous rice, rinsed thoroughly and soaked in cold water overnight

1 cup plus 2 tsp (250 ml) full-fat coconut milk

1 cup plus 2 tsp (250 ml) water

1 tsp salt

2 tsp (10 ml) pandan extract

FILLING

3 oz (84 g) dried shrimp (hebi; see Tips)

¼ cup (60 ml) water

7 oz (196 g) unsweetened desiccated coconut

3 tbsp (45 ml) rice bran, canola or grapeseed oil, plus more as needed

2 cloves garlic, minced

2 large red Asian shallots, finely chopped

2 medium stalks lemongrass (white parts only), finely chopped

2 tsp (8 g) sugar

1 tsp ground turmeric

1½ tsp (8 g) salt

12 (7 x 2-inch [18 x 5-cm]) banana leaves, passed over a gas flame until softened or blanched in boiling water until softened and patted dry (see Tips)

To make the sticky rice, combine the rice, coconut milk, water, salt and pandan in a rice cooker and cook the rice on the normal rice setting. Turn off the rice cooker and allow the rice to rest for 15 minutes to continue steaming and absorbing any remaining liquid.

In the meantime, make the filling. Soak the dried shrimp in the water for 15 minutes. Drain the shrimp and reserve the soaking liquid. Finely chop the shrimp.

In a dry, medium skillet over medium heat, toast the coconut for 4 to 5 minutes, or until it is golden brown. Transfer the coconut to a plate to cool.

Heat the oil in the skillet over medium heat. Add the garlic, shallots, lemongrass and shrimp. Cook the mixture for 2 to 3 minutes, until the ingredients are soft and fragrant. Add the coconut, sugar, turmeric and salt and mix thoroughly. Add all the soaking liquid from the shrimp. Stir-fry the mixture for 2 to 3 minutes, until it comes together in a coarse paste. Remove the filling from the heat and allow it to cool.

Lay out a banana leaf, dull side up, and brush it lightly with some additional oil. Place 2 to 3 tablespoons (20 to 30 g) of the rice on the lower half of the leaf. Leave about 1 inch (2.5 cm) of space on either side of the rice. Flatten the rice down slightly until it is 5 inches (13 cm) long, then spoon a strip of the filling along the center of the rice. Roll the banana leaf up from the edge closest to you, rolling the rice over so it encases the filling completely. Roll the leaf tightly and secure the ends with office staples or toothpicks. Repeat this process with the remaining banana leaves, rice and filling.

Preheat the grill to medium-low heat (300°F [149°C]). Add the parcels and grill them for 10 to 15 minutes per side, until they are charred. Serve the parcels hot.

Tips : You can make a vegan version by omitting the dried shrimp or the filling all together.

Banana leaves are available at Asian supermarkets and some farmers' markets.

Banana leaves need a little preparation before they can be used to wrap food. Pass the leaves over an open flame for a few seconds until the green color deepens and the leaf becomes flexible, or blanch the leaves in boiling water. The leaves can be frozen until you want to use them.

VIETNAMESE GRILLED PORK SKEWERS
(NEM NUONG)

In my opinion, the best pork sausages are found in Vietnamese and Thai cuisine. *Nem nuong* embodies the perfect balance of meatiness, spiciness, sweetness and saltiness. The rich, savory bacon and the warm spices of cinnamon and star anise in the five-spice powder pair beautifully with the fresh, lively herbs. This recipe requires forming the sausages like little kebabs around a skewer. However, the pork mixture can also be stuffed into sausage casings.

MAKES 10 TO 12 SKEWERS

PORK SKEWERS

3 cloves garlic, finely chopped

2 large red Asian shallots, finely chopped

3 bacon belly rashers (slices), finely chopped

1 lb (450 g) 20% fat ground pork (see Tip)

2 tsp (6 g) five-spice powder

2 tbsp (18 g) cornstarch

3 tbsp (45 ml) honey

3 tbsp (45 ml) rice bran, canola or grapeseed oil, divided

2 tbsp (30 ml) fish sauce

1 tbsp (15 ml) light soy sauce

1 tbsp (15 ml) rice wine

SERVING SUGGESTIONS

Vermicelli noodles, soaked in hot water for 10 to 15 minutes and drained

Lettuce leaves

Fresh Vietnamese mint stems and leaves

Fresh cilantro stems and leaves

Spring onions, cut into 3- to 4-inch (7.5- to 10-cm) pieces

Rice paper

Vietnamese Spicy Dipping Sauce (page 127)

Soak 10 to 12 bamboo skewers in water for at least 30 minutes.

To make the pork skewers, combine the garlic, shallots and bacon in a food processor. Pulse a few times to mix the ingredients well, then process continuously until a coarse paste forms.

Transfer the paste to a large bowl. Add the pork, five-spice powder, cornstarch, honey, 2 tablespoons (30 ml) of the oil, fish sauce, soy sauce and rice wine. Use your hands to mix the ingredients thoroughly, squeezing and pressing the mixture firmly as you go, for at least 10 minutes, until everything is uniformly combined and the pork becomes smooth and tacky.

Preheat the grill to medium-high heat (400 to 450°F [204 to 232°C]).

Measure out 1 to 2 tablespoons (15 to 30 g) of the pork mixture and form it into a tight ball. Then squeeze the ball into a sausage shape about 3 to 4 inches (7.5 to 10 cm) long, and push a skewer through the center of the meat. Repeat this process with the remaining pork mixture.

Use the remaining 1 tablespoon (15 ml) of oil to brush each of the sausages. Grill them for 3 to 4 minutes on each side, until they are brown and cooked through.

Serve the skewers with accompaniments such as vermicelli noodles, lettuce leaves, herbs, spring onions, rice paper and Vietnamese Spicy Dipping Sauce.

TIP: Note that 20 percent fat is the minimum amount of fat necessary for this recipe.

MALAYSIAN CHICKEN SATAY

Satay—specifically, Malaysian chicken satay—punctuates most of the happy family barbecues in my life. The juicy chicken pieces, which are covered in the warmth of curry spices and a hint of sweetness and then paired with a creamy peanut sauce, hold a special place in my heart. There is nothing greater than seeing the family gather around the barbecue as they flip skewers of satay, sip an icy beverage and have a good time. The marinade in this recipe works brilliantly with beef and pork too.

MAKES 22 TO 24 SKEWERS

CHICKEN SATAY

3 tbsp (27 g) curry powder

2 tsp (6 g) ground turmeric

1 tsp brown sugar

1 large onion, minced

3 cloves garlic, minced

Pinch of salt

3 tbsp (45 ml) rice bran, canola or grapeseed oil

6 (4-oz [112-g]) boneless, skinless chicken thighs, cut into bite-size pieces

SERVING SUGGESTIONS

Creamy Malaysian Peanut Sauce (page 131) or store-bought peanut sauce

Thickly sliced cucumber

Thinly sliced red onion

Soak 22 to 24 thin bamboo skewers in warm water for 30 minutes.

To make the chicken satay, mix together the curry powder, turmeric, brown sugar, onion, garlic, salt and oil in a large bowl. Add the chicken thigh pieces to the marinade and combine thoroughly. Marinate the chicken for at least 1 hour (or preferably overnight in the refrigerator).

Preheat the grill to medium-high heat (400 to 450°F [204 to 232°C]).

Thread 3 to 5 pieces of chicken onto each skewer, depending on the size of the chicken pieces. The chicken should cover only the top third of the skewers.

Grill the skewers for 2 to 3 minutes per side, then move the skewers to medium heat (350°F [177°C]) and cook the skewers for a further 2 to 3 minutes per side, until the chicken is opaque all the way through when cut open.

Serve the satay skewers with the Creamy Malaysian Peanut Sauce, cucumber and red onion.

GRILLED MUSSELS WITH LIME AND PEPPER SAUCE
(TUK MERIC)

I will never forget the first experience of the overwhelmingly fruity and spicy kick of Cambodia's Kampot black pepper. Mostly because it was delicious, but also because I was in the remote province of Preah Vihear (near the border of Thailand and Laos) and didn't realize I was eating pepper-coated frog legs! Pepper offers such an exciting depth of flavor and texture. We often add only a sprinkle or a shake to dishes, so when I discovered pepper being used abundantly as the main flavoring for many dishes and sauces in Cambodia, I was completely taken by surprise. This dish is one of my absolute favorites on the barbecue and a tribute to the magical pairing of Cambodian pepper and seafood. There is nothing better than plump, juicy shellfish paired with this tangy, fragrant and peppery Cambodian sauce called *tuk meric*.

SERVES 2 TO 3

4 tbsp (36 g) black peppercorns, toasted and finely ground

2 tsp (10 g) salt

2 tsp (6 g) brown sugar

½ cup (120 ml) fresh lime juice

2 lbs (900 g) fresh mussels in the shells, cleaned (see Tips)

1 to 2 tbsp (15 to 30 ml) rice bran, canola or grapeseed oil

Thinly sliced fresh cilantro leaves, as needed

Preheat the grill to high heat (450 to 475°F [232 to 246°C]).

In a medium bowl, mix together the peppercorns, salt, brown sugar and lime juice. Stir thoroughly until the salt and sugar are dissolved. Set the sauce aside.

Place the mussels on the grill and close the grill's lid, or place a large metal bowl over the top of the mussels to trap the steam and smoke. Cook the mussels for 2 to 3 minutes. Check to see if all the mussels have opened. If not, cook them for another 1 to 2 minutes. Remove the mussels from the heat as quickly as you can and transfer them to a large bowl. Discard any mussels that have not opened.

While the mussels are still hot, dress them with the sauce and oil. Sprinkle the cilantro over the mussels and serve immediately.

Tips: Always ensure your mussels are fresh before cooking by asking your fishmonger, and making sure there are no offensive smells or broken shells.

The mussels can be replaced with clams or other shellfish. The sauce works beautifully with most seafood!

STREET MARKET BITES

The best way to get to know a new place is through food. The street food markets in Southeast Asia are the perfect place to understand the region's people, flavors and charm. The markets are where I learned to taste, smell and enjoy everything that looks, sounds or smells intriguing and unique. Immersing myself in the markets is a liberating experience that has led to friendships with produce and stall vendors.

The recipes in this chapter all represent lighter snacks that are meant for grazing. Just like the street food markets, there are no hard-and-fast rules of when or what to eat. Malaysian Flatbread (page 69) is delicious with the shared plates of the next chapter, such as spicy, sultry Sambal Eggplant (page 111) and Malaysian Beef Rendang (page 100). Crisp, light, sweet and sour Papaya Salad (page 54) is perfect with steak, barbecue or in wraps and sandwiches. These snack recipes can be whipped up any time of the year and make an impressive addition to the menu when you're cooking for friends and family.

LAOTIAN MEATBALLS

These meatballs are Laotian, the dipping sauce is Vietnamese and my first encounter with this dish was in Cambodia. I was on a medical mission to remote villages around Cambodia when I was a teenager. I had culture shock. The language, the history, the people, the medical work, the traffic: it was all overwhelming for a teenager without much travel exposure. While I eventually fell in love with Cambodia, during that trip I relied on its unique food for comfort. These meatballs actually first appeared to me in sausage form and delighted me. They're packed with relentless herbaceousness. I hope the lemongrass- and dill-forward flavor delights you as much as it did me.

MAKES 20 TO 25 MEATBALLS

MEATBALLS

3 cloves garlic

1 small brown or yellow onion or 1 large red Asian shallot

1 spring onion

1 medium red serrano chili

1 (1½-inch [4-cm]) piece fresh galangal or ginger, grated

2 tbsp (6 g) finely chopped fresh dill

1 medium stalk lemongrass

1 lb (450 g) 10% fat ground pork (see Tips)

1½ tsp (8 g) salt

Pinch of ground black pepper

1 tsp sugar

1¼ tsp (4 g) ground turmeric

5 tbsp (75 ml) rice bran, canola or grapeseed oil, divided

1 tbsp (9 g) cornstarch

SERVING SUGGESTIONS

Vietnamese Spicy Dipping Sauce (page 127)

Mixed lettuce leaves (such as romaine, iceberg and oakleaf)

To make the meatballs, combine the garlic, onion, spring onion, serrano chili, galangal, dill and lemongrass in a food processor. Pulse until the ingredients are minced.

Transfer the minced vegetables to a large bowl. Add the pork, salt, black pepper, sugar, turmeric, 1 tablespoon (15 ml) of the oil and cornstarch. Knead the mixture with your hands for 5 to 6 minutes, squeezing and pressing the pork until it becomes sticky and holds together in one lump. If the mixture is too crumbly, continue kneading until it becomes a uniform mixture with no obvious lumps of ground meat. Alternatively, combine the ingredients in a large food processor and pulse until the ingredients come together as one mass.

Ideally, let the meat rest for at least 30 minutes to absorb all the flavors. If necessary, the meat is ready to use immediately after mixing.

Shape meatballs out of the mixture that are about 1 inch (2.5 cm) in diameter.

Heat the remaining 4 tablespoons (60 ml) of oil in a large skillet over medium-high heat. Working in batches if necessary, add the meatballs and fry them for 6 to 7 minutes, rolling the meatballs every 30 seconds to develop a brown crust. Let the meatballs rest for 5 minutes before serving them with the Vietnamese Spicy Dipping Sauce and lettuce leaves.

Tips: Note that 10 percent fat is the minimum amount of fat necessary for this recipe. Try to get ground pork that is as high in fat as you can. The higher the fat percentage, the juicier the meatballs. Twenty to 30 percent fat is ideal.

The meat mixture can be prepared and formed into meatballs a day ahead—just keep it covered and refrigerated.

You may need to fry the meatballs in batches. Don't overcrowd the skillet, as this will inhibit any browning and cause the meatballs to steam rather than fry and develop a nice crust.

Skewering the meatballs or stuffing the mixture into sausage casings and grilling the sausages on a barbecue is another excellent way to serve these. The smokiness really adds to the flavor! Alternatively, form the pork mixture around a skewer.

VIETNAMESE CRISPY SPRING ROLLS
(CHA GIÒ)

Fried spring rolls are a temptation of mine! I can't resist the moreish crunch, oily satisfaction and steaming-hot filling. During all my travels, spring rolls have been a go-to street snack. One of my favorites is the Vietnamese-style *cha giò*. The outer layer of rice paper bubbles and looks like layers of transparent puff pastry! These spring rolls look and feel impressive, but they are deceptively simple to make. You can replace the prawns with crabmeat and substitute the pork with ground chicken, if desired. I love the classic prawn and pork filling, but crab comes in as a close second!

SERVES 4

FILLING

3 oz (84 g) dry mung bean thread noodles (also known as glass noodles)

6 to 8 fresh large prawns, shelled, deveined, tails removed and meat coarsely chopped

9 oz (252 g) 20% fat ground pork (see Tip)

2 large red Asian shallots or 1 small brown or yellow onion, finely chopped

2 cloves garlic, minced

1 tbsp (9 g) cornstarch

2 tbsp (30 ml) fish sauce

1 tsp sugar

1 tsp ground black pepper

1 tsp salt

1 large egg

WRAPPERS

20 (8- to 10-inch [20- to 25-cm]) dry rice paper wrappers

2 tsp (8 g) sugar dissolved in 1 cup (240 ml) hot water, cooled

Rice bran, canola or grapeseed oil, as needed

SERVING SUGGESTIONS

Lettuce leaves

Fresh mint leaves with stems

Fresh cilantro leaves with stems

Thinly sliced chilies (any variety)

Vietnamese Spicy Dipping Sauce (page 127)

To make the filling, soak the noodles in very hot water for 3 to 4 minutes, until they are soft and transparent. Rinse the noodles in cold water and wrap them in a clean tea towel. Twist and squeeze the towel lightly to soak up any excess water from the noodles. Transfer the noodles to a large bowl and cut them into 1-inch (2.5-cm)-long strands with kitchen scissors.

Add the prawns to the noodles. Crumble the pork into the noodles, then add the shallots, garlic, cornstarch, fish sauce, sugar, black pepper, salt and egg. Mix until the ingredients are well combined.

To make the wrappers, set out a large plate or tray next to the bowl of filling. Line a second large plate or tray with parchment paper and set it next to the first one. Dunk one-third of a wrapper into the sugar-water mixture. Place the wrapper on the plate and use your hand to spread the water on one-third of the wrapper to the rest of it. The wrapper should not be soaking wet, but it should be wet enough that it becomes pliable.

Working quickly, place 2 tablespoons (30 g) of filling on the bottom half of the wrapper. Fold the left and right sides of the wrapper over, then roll the wrapper from the bottom up to form a spring roll. Place the spring roll onto the second plate. Repeat the filling and folding process with the remaining wrappers and filling. Let all of the spring rolls air-dry for at least 15 minutes and use paper towels to soak up any excess moisture on the surface of the rolls. Alternatively, you can fold all of the spring rolls a few hours in advance and refrigerate them for 2 to 3 hours to allow them to dry out.

Fill a large saucepan half full with the oil. Heat the oil to 325°F (163°C). Working in batches so as not to overcrowd the saucepan, fry the spring rolls for about 2 minutes, until they are golden. Transfer the spring rolls to paper towels to drain. If desired, slice the spring rolls into bite-size pieces.

Serve the spring rolls with the lettuce, mint, cilantro, chilies and Vietnamese Spicy Dipping Sauce.

TIP: Note that 20 percent fat is the minimum amount of fat necessary for this recipe. The higher the fat percentage, the juicier the filling will be. Twenty to 30 percent fat is ideal.

VIETNAMESE PANCAKES WITH PORK AND PRAWNS
(BÁNH XÈO)

Bánh xèo translates to "sizzling pancake" in Vietnamese. These vibrant yellow pancakes have a subtle turmeric flavor, but the filling is where this dish shines! Pork strips and prawns are a typical combination, but once you get the hang of the pancake batter, you can customize the filling to any combination you want. In Vietnam, this dish is served with rice paper, lettuce leaves and fresh herbs. It seems unusual to wrap pancakes with something else, but it is an absolutely delicious way to eat them.

MAKES 4 TO 5 PANCAKES

BATTER

1 cup (150 g) rice flour

⅓ cup (40 g) all-purpose flour

1 to 1½ cups (240 to 360 ml) water, plus more as needed

2 tsp (6 g) ground turmeric

Salt, as needed

Ground white pepper, as needed

FILLING

Rice bran, canola or grapeseed oil, as needed

1 medium onion, finely chopped

2 cloves garlic, finely chopped

4 to 5 oz (112 to 140 g) pork neck, cut into thin strips

2 tbsp (30 ml) light soy sauce

12 to 15 large prawns, shelled and deveined

1 small bundle bok choy, mustard greens or kohlrabi leaves, thinly sliced

1 to 2 tbsp (8 to 16 g) shredded jicama

½ medium red serrano chili or 1 small bird's eye chili, thinly sliced

7 oz (196 g) fresh bean sprouts

SERVING SUGGESTIONS

Fresh mint, dill and cilantro leaves

Vietnamese Spicy Dipping Sauce (page 127)

To make the batter, combine the rice flour, all-purpose flour, water, turmeric, salt and white pepper in a large bowl. Whisk the ingredients together until the batter is smooth. The batter should be runnier than pancake batter but remain separated when you coat the back of a spoon with it and trace a line through it with your finger. You can add more water to loosen the mixture or add more flour to thicken it.

To make the filling, heat 1 tablespoon (15 ml) of the oil in a large skillet over medium-high heat. Add the onion, garlic and pork and cook them for 2 to 3 minutes, until they are caramelized. Add the soy sauce and toss to coat all the meat.

Add the prawns and bok choy to the pork mixture. Stir-fry the mixture for 2 to 3 minutes, until the prawns have changed to a bright orange color.

Turn off the heat, then add the jicama and chili and mix well. Transfer the mixture to a large bowl and set it aside.

Heat 2 teaspoons (10 ml) of the oil in a clean, medium non-stick skillet over medium heat. Pour in about ¼ cup (60 ml) of the batter while simultaneously rolling the pan in a circular motion to spread the batter all around. Try to make a thin pancake that's relatively even in thickness. Cook the pancake for 3 to 4 minutes, or until it is crispy and starting to brown on the bottom.

Once the upward-facing surface of the pancake becomes solid and opaque, spoon approximately 3 tablespoons (45 g) of the filling onto one half of the pancake. Top the filling with a few of the bean sprouts, then fold the other half of the pancake over the filling. Press down lightly on the pancake. Cook the filled pancake for 1 minute.

Repeat the preceding steps with the remaining batter and filling. Serve the pancakes with the mint, dill and cilantro and Vietnamese Spicy Dipping Sauce.

PAPAYA SALAD
(SOM TUM)

Thanks to the sweltering heat and high humidity, papaya salad is a staple across Southeast Asia. The sharp sourness of the limes, the cool crunch of the green papaya and the juiciness of the tomatoes create a light, refreshing dish. In Thailand, it's amazing how different this salad, called *som tum*, is from food stall to food stall. The beauty of this salad, like a lot of dishes in Southeast Asian cuisines, is that you can customize the seasonings to your preferred level of sourness, saltiness and sweetness. For me, this dish was a revelation of the spirit of Southeast Asian cooking: It is personal yet expressive and does not always play by the rules.

SERVES 4

PAPAYA SALAD

1 clove garlic

2 long snake beans or 6 green beans, cut into 2-inch (5-cm) pieces

6 cherry tomatoes, halved

2 whole small Thai red chilies

½ large green papaya, peeled, seeded and shredded (see Tip)

1 tbsp (15 g) dried shrimp (hebi), soaked for 10 minutes in warm water, drained and finely chopped

1 tbsp (15 ml) fish sauce

Juice of 1 medium lime

1 tsp sugar

SERVING SUGGESTIONS

2 tbsp (16 g) crushed roasted peanuts (optional)

Thai sticky rice, cooked per packet instructions

Place the garlic in a large mortar or sturdy plastic or metal bowl and use a pestle or potato masher to crush the garlic. Then add the snake beans, cherry tomatoes and chilies to the garlic and crush everything lightly.

Add the papaya, shrimp, fish sauce, lime juice and sugar to the mortar and continue to crush the ingredients lightly while intermittently mixing them with a spoon or spatula. Once the ingredients are combined well, taste and adjust the seasoning to your preference. Top the salad with the peanuts (if using) and serve with the sticky rice.

TIP: Shred the papaya using a mandoline or papaya shredder. Alternatively, you can use a food processor to shred the papaya or simply use a knife to cut the papaya into very thin matchsticks.

CRISPY ONION FRITTERS (PAKORAS)
AND CILANTRO-YOGURT SAUCE

I first came across Crispy Onion Fritters in Kuala Lumpur, Malaysia, when I was a child. My cousin handed me a greasy paper bag. Stacked inside were these deep-fried fritters that looked wild and spidery. Biting into one was sensational. There was the sweetness from the onion, the crunchy nuttiness from the chickpea flour and the blasts of flavor from the spice mix. These are best eaten hot and crispy, as they don't keep well in the refrigerator after they've been fried.

MAKES 12 TO 15 PAKORAS

GARAM MASALA

2 tbsp (10 g) coriander seeds

10 cardamom pods or ½ tsp ground cardamom

2 (3-inch [7.5-cm]) cinnamon sticks

6 cloves

1 star anise pod

3 tsp (6 g) cumin seeds

10 dried mild red chilies (such as guajillos)

PAKORAS

2 large onions

1½ tsp (8 g) salt

2 tsp (6 g) red pepper flakes

2 cups (260 g) chickpea flour

1 tsp baking powder

1 cup (240 ml) water, or as needed

4 to 5 cups (960 ml to 1.2 L) rice bran, canola or grapeseed oil

½ lemon, cut into wedges

CILANTRO-YOGURT SAUCE

½ cup (120 g) plain unsweetened yogurt (see Tips)

Juice of ½ medium lemon

12 fresh mint leaves with stems, thinly sliced

1 cup (50 g) coarsely chopped fresh cilantro

Salt, as needed

To make the garam masala, combine the coriander seeds, cardamom pods (if using whole pods), cinnamon sticks, cloves, star anise and cumin seeds in a medium skillet over low heat. Toast the spices for 4 to 5 minutes, or until they become fragrant and they darken in color. Let the spices cool for 10 minutes.

Combine the toasted spices and the chilies in a spice grinder and process until they form a fine powder. Stir in the ground cardamom if you are using it instead of pods.

Keep the spice mix in an airtight container. Store leftovers in a dry place for up to 3 months.

To make the pakoras, slice the onions about ¼ inch (6 mm) thick.

Place the sliced onions into a large bowl. Add 2 teaspoons (6 g) of the garam masala, salt and red pepper flakes. Mix the ingredients well, separating the pieces of onion as you go. Add the chickpea flour and baking powder. Mix the ingredients thoroughly.

Begin to add the water gradually, mixing thoroughly as you add it. Once the mixture is well combined, set it aside for 10 to 15 minutes to allow the chickpea flour to hydrate. The texture should be like thick pancake batter. (You may find you don't need all the water, or you need more. You want the batter thick enough to hold the onion pieces together, but thin enough so that it coats all the pieces of onion.)

While the flour mixture hydrates, prepare the cilantro-yogurt sauce. In a blender, combine the yogurt, lemon juice, mint and cilantro. Blend until the ingredients are well combined and the sauce is a gorgeous shade of green. The sauce should be a little runny. Taste and season the sauce with salt.

Add the oil to a large saucepan. Heat the oil to between 360 and 370°F (182 and 188°C). Add 4 tablespoons (60 ml) of the hot oil straight into the onion mixture and mix thoroughly.

Using a spoon, press together clusters of the onions and batter together so they form a round dumpling shape. Working in batches of 4 to 6 so as not to overcrowd the pan, carefully drop the pakoras into the oil. Fry the pakoras for 3 to 4 minutes, until the pakoras are a rich golden brown. Flip them halfway through the cooking time if needed. Drain the pakoras on a wire rack.

Serve the pakoras with the cilantro-yogurt sauce and lemon wedges.

Tips: You can add other vegetables, sliced very thinly, to the pakora mixture (e.g., jalapeños, carrots and bell peppers).

To make this vegan, substitute the dairy-based yogurt with vegan yogurt.

THAI FISH CAKES
(TOD MUN PLA)

The bouncy, springy texture of these fish cakes is sublime. A lot of Southeast Asian food is a textural experience. Southeast Asians love chewy, soft, bouncy, sticky foods. The fish cakes in Bangkok are slightly greasy on the outside from being fried, and once you bite through to the toothsome center, there's a burst of spicy red curry flavor and a satisfying crunch from the beans. Dipped into sticky, sweet chili sauce, these are a perfect snack.

MAKES 10 TO 12 FISH CAKES

SWEET CHILI SAUCE

3 cloves garlic

2 medium red serrano chilies or other moderately hot red chilies, coarsely chopped, seeds optional

1 small bird's eye or Thai chili or one small hot chili, seeds optional

5 tbsp (60 g) sugar

½ tsp salt

⅓ cup (80 ml) distilled white vinegar

¼ cup (60 ml) water

FISH CAKES

1 lb (450 g) soft, skinless whitefish fillet (such as sole, basa, cod, orange roughy)

2 to 3 tbsp (30 to 45 g) red curry paste

1 tsp sugar

2 large red Asian shallots, finely chopped

2 tsp (10 ml) fish sauce

½ cup (85 g) finely chopped snake beans

15 fresh Thai basil or holy basil leaves, thinly sliced

5 fresh kaffir lime leaves, very thinly sliced

Rice bran, canola or grapeseed oil, as needed

To make the sweet chili sauce, combine the garlic, serrano chilies, bird's eye chili, sugar, salt, vinegar and water in a blender and blend until the ingredients are smooth. Transfer the mixture to a small saucepan over medium heat. Simmer the sauce for 7 to 8 minutes, until it has reduced and slightly thickened. Remove the sauce from the heat and allow it to cool. It will continue to thicken as it cools. If you prefer a thinner texture, mix in 1 tablespoon (15 ml) of water at a time until the sauce reaches your desired consistency.

To make the fish cakes, combine the fish, curry paste, sugar, shallots and fish sauce in a food processor. Process, scraping down the sides of the food processor bowl as needed, until the mixture is smooth and thick enough to hold its shape. It should resemble thick mashed potatoes.

Transfer the fish mixture to a large bowl. Add the beans, Thai basil leaves and kaffir lime leaves. Mix the ingredients together thoroughly.

Fill a large, deep skillet with just under ½ inch (13 mm) of oil. Heat the oil over medium-high heat.

While the oil heats, wet your hands and form the fish mixture into 10 to 12 patty-shaped fish cakes. Set the fish cakes aside on a large plate or tray. Re-wet your hands as needed while you form the fish cakes.

Working in batches so as not to overcrowd the skillet, add the fish cakes to the oil. Cook them for about 2 to 3 minutes on each side, or until they are deeply browned on both sides. Remove the fish cakes from the skillet and allow them to drain on paper towels.

Serve the fish cakes with the sweet chili sauce.

DRUNKEN CLAMS

One of my favorite things to eat in Kuala Lumpur, Malaysia, is drunken clams. You typically find them in Chinese restaurants, and they're made with cooking wine. However, sometimes the cooking wine is a little too bitter and harsh, so I've updated this quick and easy recipe with beer for the perfect Aussie twist! It's a great starter for barbecues or summer get-togethers.

SERVES 2 TO 3

CLAMS

2 tbsp (30 ml) rice bran, canola or grapeseed oil

2 large red Asian shallots, diced

2 cloves garlic, thinly sliced

3 medium red serrano chilies, thinly sliced

4½ lbs (2 kg) fresh clams or cockles, cleaned (see Tips)

12 oz (360 ml) lager beer (see Tips)

Juice of ½ medium lemon

2 spring onions, thinly sliced

SERVING SUGGESTIONS

Cold beer

Thai sticky rice, cooked per packet instructions, or bread

To make the clams, heat the oil in a large skillet or wok over medium-high heat until the oil is slightly smoking. Add the shallots, garlic and serrano chilies. Stir-fry the mixture for 1 to 2 minutes, until the garlic and shallots begin to caramelize.

Add the clams and toss them quickly once or twice. Add the beer and cover the skillet with a lid. Cook the clams for about 2 minutes, shaking the skillet every 30 to 40 seconds. Remove the lid and add the lemon juice and spring onions. The clams should all be open—discard any that are not. Shake the skillet again to thoroughly mix everything and remove the skillet from the heat.

Serve the clams with cold beer and sticky rice or bread to dip into the juices.

TIPS: Discard any clams that are open or have broken shells before cooking.

If you don't care for lager beer, use cider or another type of beer with a sweet flavor profile.

PRAWN TOAST

On a weekend in Malaysia, I love sleeping in then kicking off the balmy morning with these crispy Prawn Toasts and an icy, bittersweet coffee. These toasts are greasy and savory in a decadent way, but the sesame flavor and zing of ginger lighten them up. I've added crispy curry leaves for texture and a distinctive aroma that gives warmth to the dish. Add this recipe to your brunch repertoire!

SERVES 4

6 to 8 raw prawns, shells removed and deveined

2 cloves garlic, grated

1 (1½-inch [4-cm]) piece fresh ginger, grated

1 tsp toasted sesame oil

Ground black pepper, as needed

Salt, as needed

4 thick slices white sandwich bread or brioche, cut into thirds

2 to 3 tbsp (20 to 30 g) untoasted white sesame seeds

Rice bran, canola or grapeseed oil, as needed

15 to 20 fresh curry leaves, stems removed

In a food processor, combine the prawns, garlic, ginger, sesame oil, black pepper and salt. Process the mixture until it becomes a fine paste.

If desired, remove the crusts from the slices of bread. Place the sesame seeds on a plate. Spread a thick layer of the prawn paste onto each slice of bread, then dip the prawn side into the sesame seeds.

Heat about 1 inch (2.5 cm) of oil in a medium skillet over medium heat. Add the curry leaves to the oil, being careful as you do so because they will spit and pop. Cook the curry leaves for 10 seconds, until they are translucent and crispy. Remove them from the oil using a frying spider or strainer and transfer them to paper towels to drain.

Add the prawn toast to the hot oil, prawn side down. Fry the toast for 1 to 2 minutes, until it is a golden color. Flip the toast and fry the other side of the bread for 1 to 2 minutes, until it is crunchy and golden. Remove the prawn toasts from the oil and let them drain on paper towels before serving.

Serve the prawn toasts topped with the crispy curry leaves.

SON-IN-LAW EGGS

No one really knows the true story behind the name of these deliciously crispy, spicy and tangy eggs, but I've heard a particularly colorful urban legend from the streets of Bangkok. A woman had concerns that her daughter was being mistreated by her son-in-law. She deep-fried eggs and served them with a spicy, sour sauce to send a bold message: If he wasn't careful, his 'family jewels' would be deep-fried! (I'd say the woman was a rather clever cook.) Regardless of its origins, this dish is addictive with its mouthwatering sauce and creamy egg yolks. These eggs make a great lunchbox snack for the next day too.

MAKES 2 SERVINGS

Salt, as needed

4 large eggs

1 cup (240 ml) rice bran, canola or grapeseed oil

3 large red Asian shallots, thinly sliced

2 cloves garlic, thinly sliced

4 dried red chilies (such as chile de árbols or guajillos), cut into roughly 1-inch (2.5-cm) pieces

3 tbsp (45 g) tamarind paste

1 tbsp (9 g) grated palm sugar or brown sugar

1 tbsp (15 ml) fish sauce

Coarsely chopped fresh cilantro, as needed

Fill a medium saucepan with water and bring it to a boil over high heat. Add a generous amount of salt to the water. Once the salt has dissolved, carefully lower the eggs into the water and boil them for 6 minutes.

In the meantime, fill a large bowl with ice water. Transfer the boiled eggs to the ice water immediately. Leave them to chill.

Heat the oil in a medium wok or skillet over medium heat. Add the shallots and fry them for 3 to 4 minutes, until they are golden brown. Transfer the shallots to paper towels to drain.

Add the garlic and chilies to the oil and fry them until the garlic is golden brown, about 2 to 3 minutes. Remove the garlic and chilies and transfer them to the paper towels to drain with the shallots.

The eggs should now be very cold. Peel them carefully and then pat them dry with paper towels. Keep the peeled eggs whole. Increase the heat on the stove to medium-high. Add the eggs and fry them for 2 to 3 minutes, or until they are golden and blistered all over. Remove the eggs from the oil and transfer them to paper towels to drain.

Pour most of the oil from the wok into a heatproof bowl or jar, leaving 3 to 4 tablespoons (45 to 60 ml) of oil in the wok. (You can keep the reserved oil and use it for other recipes, as it has been flavored with the shallots, garlic and chilies.) Place the wok over medium heat.

Add the tamarind paste, sugar and fish sauce to the wok. Stir-fry this mixture for 10 to 12 minutes, until it is well combined, thick and jammy. Remove the wok from the heat when you've reached the desired consistency.

Slice the eggs in half and arrange them on a plate. Top the eggs with the tamarind sauce and garnish them with the fried shallots, chilies and garlic and fresh cilantro.

CAMBODIAN "SHAKING BEEF" SALAD
(LOC LAC KHMER)

I was first introduced to this simple dish in Phnom Penh. I had just finished a long day cataloging and packing medical supplies into crates and vans for a medical mission into rural villages of Cambodia. With both exhaustion and excitement humming away in our bones, our mission group stopped for dinner at an outdoor food court. I distinctly remember the growling motorbikes and people yelling from stall to stall. One of the local guides staying with us encouraged me to try "shaking beef" from a rowdy chef. "*Loc lac! Loc lac!*" the chef called out as he tossed beef around the wok. A peppery, sweet and sour aroma was rising out of it. He plated the steaming-hot beef strips on a large piece of lettuce and added thick slices of tomatoes, a pile of raw onions and a little plastic cup of lime juice and black pepper. This recipe is a twist of that simple, comforting dish. I've made it into a hearty salad that still captures the signature Khmer lime and pepper flavor.

SERVES 4

SALAD

1 lb (450 g) beef rump or topside, cut into ½-inch (13-mm)-wide strips

1 tbsp (15 ml) light soy sauce

1 tbsp (15 ml) fish sauce

2 tsp (4 g) ground black pepper

1 tbsp (9 g) cornstarch

½ cup (120 ml) rice bran, canola or grapeseed oil, plus more as needed

4 large red Asian shallots, thinly sliced

2 cloves garlic, thinly sliced

2 tbsp (30 g) tomato paste

1 large egg

10 oz (280 g) iceberg or romaine lettuce leaves or spinach leaves

1 cup (200 g) halved cherry, cocktail or grape tomatoes

1 cup (120 g) julienned cucumber

1 medium white or red onion, very thinly sliced

DRESSING

Juice of 1 medium lime

2 tsp (4 g) ground black pepper

1 tbsp (15 ml) fish sauce

½ tsp sugar

To make the salad, combine the beef, soy sauce, fish sauce, black pepper and cornstarch in a large bowl. Mix the ingredients together thoroughly to ensure the beef is well coated. Set the bowl aside.

Heat the oil in a medium wok over medium heat. Add the shallots and fry them for 3 to 4 minutes, until they are golden. Transfer the shallots to paper towels to drain.

Carefully transfer the majority of the oil from the wok into a medium heatproof bowl, leaving 2 to 3 tablespoons (30 to 45 ml) of oil in the wok. Reserve the bowl of oil and place the wok over medium-high heat.

Once the oil begins to smoke, add the beef, spreading it out in a single layer. Fry the beef for 1 to 2 minutes. Flip the beef and add the garlic. Fry the beef for 1 to 2 minutes, then use a spatula or wooden spoon to stir it briefly. Add the tomato paste and stir-fry the mixture for another 1 to 2 minutes, until the tomato paste becomes saucy and evenly coats all the beef. Turn off the heat and transfer the beef to a medium bowl.

Heat about 1 inch (2.5 cm) of fresh oil in another medium wok over medium-high heat. While the oil heats, crack the egg into a small bowl. When the oil begins to smoke, carefully pour the egg into the center of the wok and fry it, undisturbed, for 20 seconds. Using a spatula or ladle, baste the top of the egg with the hot oil. When the egg is set on the top, the yolk is still runny and the edges are deep golden brown, remove the egg from the wok with a slotted spoon and transfer it to paper towels to drain. Alternatively, fry the egg sunny-side up.

To make the dressing, add the lime juice, black pepper, fish sauce and sugar to the reserved shallot oil. Stir until the sugar dissolves.

In a large bowl, mix together the lettuce leaves, tomatoes, cucumber, onion, beef and dressing. Serve the salad topped with the fried shallots and fried egg.

MALAYSIAN FLATBREAD
(ROTI CANAI)

The acrobatic, skillful swinging of *roti* (bread) dough into a gossamer-thin sheet is an iconic and impressive sight in Malaysia. It was magical when I first saw it happen as a toddler. The smell of butter and the theatrics drew me in immediately. Now, as a cook, I understand that it's more than just a show. The flipping and swinging of the dough stretches it as thin as possible. When you roll it all up and cook it, it turns into hundreds of flaky, crispy layers. Since my dough-swinging skills are less than masterful, this recipe uses a simple technique of pressing the dough out as thin as you can with your palm. This recipe takes a while to master, but making your own bread is addictive and highly satisfying.

MAKES 6 ROTI

2 tsp (10 g) salt

2 tsp (8 g) sugar

¾ cup plus 4 tsp (200 ml) warm water

2¼ cups (286 g) bread flour or all-purpose flour

Rice bran, canola or grapeseed oil or ghee (clarified butter), as needed

In a small bowl, dissolve the salt and sugar in the warm water, stirring thoroughly. Let the water cool down to room temperature.

Place the flour in a large bowl. Add the water to the flour and begin kneading gently in the bowl to form a dough. Continue gently kneading for 6 to 7 minutes, or until the dough becomes smooth and no dry bits of flour are apparent.

Oil a large, deep dish or tray. Divide the dough into 6 even portions. Roll the portions into smooth balls with your hands. Add the balls to the prepared dish and then pour oil or ghee over them until they are fully submerged. Let the dough rest for at least 2 hours. (For best results, rest the dough overnight in the refrigerator.)

Take a single portion of the dough out of the oil and flatten it on a clean, dry surface. Use your palms to gently spread the dough out into a square until you can see the surface beneath it. (The square doesn't have to be perfect.) Continue pushing to stretch the dough as thin as you can get it without tearing. Little air pockets should start forming in the dough.

Once the dough is thin, roll it up like a scroll. Then take one end and roll it inward so that the scroll becomes a snail-like spiral. Gently flatten the spiral down into a large circle. Repeat this process with the remaining dough. Reserve the oil or ghee for later cooking use.

Once all the dough has been formed, heat a large skillet over medium heat. Add a drizzle of the oil that the dough was submerged in. Place 1 dough circle into the skillet, ensuring the dough makes as much contact with the skillet as possible by softly pressing down on it with a spatula. Fry the roti for 2 to 3 minutes, or until it is golden brown. Flip the roti and fry it for another 2 to 3 minutes, or until it is golden brown.

Once you remove the roti from the skillet, use your hands to "clap" the dough together. Place your hands on either side of the roti and clap several times, crushing the dough so that the layers separate and become fluffy. Repeat this process with all the roti.

TIP: The roti is typically served with chicken curry, but it's also fantastic with my Coconut Prawns (page 99) and Malaysian Beef Rendang (page 100). The dough can be made 1 day in advance.

MALAYSIAN TURMERIC LACE PANCAKES
(ROTI JALA)

These are thin, delicate lace pancakes of aromatic turmeric and coconut used to mop up delicious rendang sauce and wrap around the tender morsels of meat. What a joy to eat! During an Easter holiday to Kuala Lumpur, Malaysia, my family stopped by a roadside durian stall, keen for the smelly yet unctuous and delicious fruit. What we didn't expect was the tiny Malay stall next to the durian stall serving *rendang* and *roti jala*. The mouthwatering aroma was too good to refuse. My brother was insistent on trying these lacy little pancakes, and we were glad we did. Years later, re-creating this pancake would earn me a place on *MasterChef Australia*. I made these extra crispy and served them with coconut and lemon ice cream. Try serving it with Malaysian Beef Rendang (page 100) or ice cream.

MAKES 24 PANCAKES

2½ cups (300 g) all-purpose flour

1 tsp ground turmeric

1 tsp salt

6 tbsp (90 ml) full-fat coconut milk

1 cup (240 ml) water, plus more as needed

2 large eggs

2 tbsp (30 ml) rice bran, canola or grapeseed oil, plus more as needed

In a large bowl, sift together the flour, turmeric and salt. Mix the ingredients together thoroughly. In a medium bowl, whisk together the coconut milk, water, eggs and oil.

Whisk the coconut milk mixture into the flour mixture until a smooth pancake batter forms. If the mixture is too thick, add 1 tablespoon (15 ml) of water at a time until you reach the right consistency. The batter should fall in a continuous ribbon off the whisk when you lift it. Leave the batter to rest for 10 to 15 minutes before whisking it quickly and transferring it to a squeeze bottle.

Heat a medium nonstick skillet over medium heat and brush the surface with 1 or 2 teaspoons (5 to 10 ml) of oil. Then, using the squeeze bottle, trace a loopy, lacy, circular pattern with the batter on the bottom of the skillet.

Cook the pancake for 1 to 2 minutes on the one side, or until the pancake is dry to the touch and its edges begin to curl up from the surface of the skillet. Using a spatula, fold in the sides of the pancake and roll up the pancake like a spring roll.

Shake the squeeze bottle to remix the batter and repeat this process until all the batter is gone.

TIPS: The batter can be made a day ahead.

These pancakes can be made sweet by reducing the salt to ¼ teaspoon and adding 1 to 2 teaspoons (4 to 8 g) of white sugar when you sift the flour in the first step.

SHARED HAWKER PLATES

Hawker carts and hawker centers in Southeast Asia are street food carts and food courts dedicated to vendors selling their most delicious specialties, hot and cooked to order. To truly eat like a local in Southeast Asia, you need to go to hawker centers. They are wildly different from Western food courts that house chain restaurants. Food is cooked fast, ingredients are at their freshest and dishes tend to represent home-style cuisine cooked by family businesses. Often, vendors will specialize in one or two particular dishes and build their reputation on repeated expertise and the perfect balance of flavors. But despite all the vendors' years of experience and high skill level, food is ridiculously cheap and widely available.

The budding chef in me spent every waking moment at hawker centers in Malaysia, as well as the surrounding food carts and markets. I tasted anything and everything and was blown away by how intensely delicious the unique ingredients of Southeast Asia are. This chapter is all about translating those incredible flavors and shared plates into dishes that can be served in your home. These recipes are intended to be enjoyed around the communal table. The smoky aroma of Malaysian Fried Rice (page 75) and the rich aroma of Coconut Prawns (page 99) will get the whole table excited.

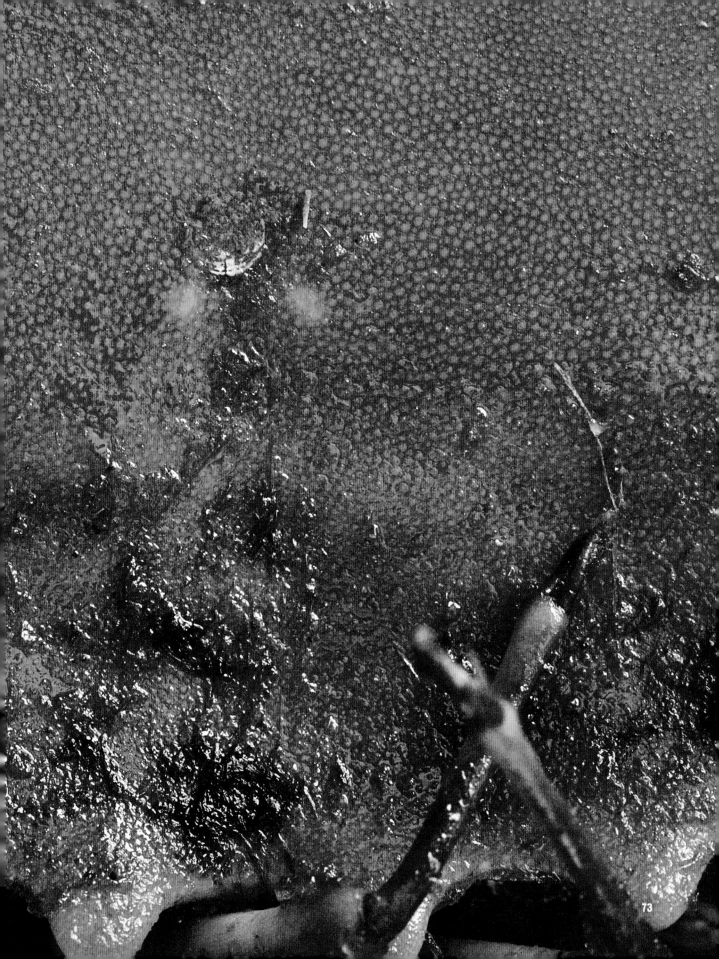

MALAYSIAN FRIED RICE
(NASI GORENG)

I worked in Kuala Lumpur, Malaysia, for a few months at the start of my career as a lawyer. It was grueling, but I always treated myself well during lunchtime. There were endless food courts and hawker centers to order from. *Nasi goreng* became one of my usual orders. It was quick, satisfying and incredibly tasty. It was also white-business-shirt-friendly! Nasi goreng became an important dish of enjoyment for me during that thirty-minute lunch break, which allowed me to unwind and recharge.

SERVES 4

MARINATED CHICKEN

5 oz (140 g) boneless, skinless chicken breast or thigh, thinly sliced (see Tips)

1 tbsp (15 ml) sweet soy sauce (kecap manis; see Tips)

1 tsp toasted sesame oil

1 tsp rice bran, canola or grapeseed oil

FRIED RICE

⅓ cup (80 ml) rice bran, canola or grapeseed oil

5 large red Asian shallots, thinly sliced, divided

2 cloves garlic, finely chopped

2 tsp (10 g) shrimp paste (belachan), crumbled

3 to 4 cups (480 to 640 g) day-old cooked white rice, chilled

2 tbsp (30 ml) sweet soy sauce (kecap manis)

1 tbsp (11 g) thinly sliced red serrano or cayenne chilies (optional)

SERVING SUGGESTIONS

4 sunny-side up fried eggs

Prawn crackers

Thinly sliced spring onions

Tomato wedges

Thinly sliced cucumber

Lime wedges

To make the marinated chicken, combine the chicken with the sweet soy sauce, sesame oil and oil in a small bowl. Mix everything together thoroughly to ensure the chicken is coated. Set the chicken aside.

To make the fried rice, heat the oil in a large wok or skillet over medium-low heat. Add 3 of the shallots. Fry the shallots, stirring occasionally, for 5 to 10 minutes or until they are golden brown. Carefully transfer the fried shallots to paper towels to drain. Keep the oil in the wok.

Increase the heat to medium-high, add the chicken and stir-fry it for 2 to 3 minutes, until it is brown and cooked through. Transfer the chicken to a plate.

Add the remaining 2 shallots and garlic to the wok. Cook them just until the garlic begins to turn golden brown, about 30 seconds. Add the shrimp paste and stir-fry the mixture for 30 seconds.

Increase the heat to high, then add the rice to the wok. (I find it easiest to use damp hands to break up the rice and crumble it into the wok.)

Stir-fry the rice for about 1 minute, until the oil and shrimp paste are evenly mixed with the rice. Add the sweet soy sauce and stir-fry the rice for 1 minute, until the sauce is well mixed with the rice. Add the chicken and chilies (if using) to the wok, and stir-fry the mixture for 1 minute, until the ingredients are well combined.

Remove the fried rice from the heat, divide into 4 bowls and serve each portion with a fried egg, prawn crackers, spring onions, tomato wedges, cucumber and lime wedges.

TIPS: You can use any protein you like and marinate it the same way as directed in this recipe. Beef or pressed firm tofu are common substitutes.

Kecap manis (sweet soy sauce) is a thickened, sweet soy sauce generally available at larger grocery stores and Asian grocery stores. You can also make your own by bringing ½ cup (120 ml) of light soy sauce and ¼ cup (36 g) of brown sugar to a simmer in a small saucepan over medium heat. Reduce the sauce for 10 to 15 minutes, or until it is almost the consistency of maple syrup. It's best to store this sauce in a glass jar at room temperature, as it will thicken and become stickier as it cools.

CRISPY PORK BELLY
(SIEW YOKE)

While crispy pork belly and rice was available at some of the hawker centers in Malaysia, my mum swears that my grandfather's was the best. Inspired by the hawkers, my grandfather developed his own recipe using the more intense flavors of five-spice powder and garlic. After immigrating to Australia, Mum had to develop her own recipe based off the memory of his. The flavors were spot-on, but this recipe uses techniques that I've learned over time. I dare say my crackling is far better than Mum's! In fact, this is one of the dishes I feature at Pork Party, my pop-up market stall in Sydney, Australia.

SERVES 5 TO 6

1 tbsp (9 g) five-spice powder

2 tsp (6 g) garlic powder

1½ tsp (8 g) salt

2 tsp (4 g) ground black pepper

2 tbsp (30 ml) rice bran, canola or grapeseed oil

2¼ lbs (1 kg) skin-on pork belly

1 to 2 cups (288 to 576 g) kosher salt

1¼ to 1½ cups (300 to 360 ml) boiling water

2 cups (420 g) uncooked rice

2 tbsp (30 ml) sweet soy sauce (kecap manis; see Tips), or store-bought

1 to 2 cloves garlic, minced

1 tbsp (15 ml) toasted sesame oil

1 lb (450 g) bok choy, quartered lengthwise

Preheat the oven to 350°F (177°C). Line a large rimmed baking sheet with foil, then place an oven-safe wire rack on the baking sheet.

In a small bowl, combine the five-spice powder, garlic powder, salt, black pepper and oil.

Using paper towels, pat the pork belly's skin and meat dry. (Ensure the skin is extremely dry.) Spread the five-spice mixture on the meat side of the pork belly, then place the pork belly, skin side up, on the rack on the prepared baking sheet.

Cover the pork belly's skin with the kosher salt, creating a thick layer of salt that covers the entire surface. Add the boiling water to the tray, then place the tray on the middle rack of the oven. Roast the pork belly for 45 minutes, until the kosher salt forms a cohesive crust.

Remove the salt crust from the pork belly. Increase the oven's temperature to 450°F (232°C) and roast the pork belly for 30 to 40 minutes, until it is crispy.

While the pork belly roasts, cook the rice per the package's instructions.

Remove the pork belly from the oven and let it rest for 15 to 20 minutes. Slice it into bite-size pieces.

While the pork belly is resting, combine the sweet soy sauce, garlic and sesame oil in a large bowl.

Bring a large pot of water to a boil over high heat. Add the bok choy and blanch it for 1 to 2 minutes, or until it is tender. Add the bok choy to the sweet soy sauce mixture and toss to coat the greens in the sauce.

Serve the pork belly with the bok choy on a bed of the rice. If desired, spoon any leftover sweet soy sauce mixture over the rice.

Tips: This dish works exceptionally well with Thai Sweet Chili Sauce (page 128), a sweet and sticky sauce.

Kecap manis (sweet soy sauce) is a thickened, sweet soy sauce generally available at larger grocery stores and Asian grocery stores. You can also make your own by bringing ½ cup (120 ml) of light soy sauce and ¼ cup (36 g) of brown sugar to a simmer in a small saucepan over medium heat. Reduce the sauce for 10 to 15 minutes, or until it is almost the consistency of maple syrup. It's best to store this sauce in a glass jar at room temperature, as it will thicken and become stickier as it cools.

SINGAPOREAN CHILI MUD CRAB

I must have been only seven or eight years old—my chin barely cleared the top of the giant round table and my feet couldn't touch the floor as I sat, surrounded by family at a local eating house serving Chinese cuisine in hot and humid Singapore. A huge platter came to our table almost overflowing with thick red sauce, and the aroma of chilies and tomatoes instantly hit my nose. Three gigantic mud crabs sat in the center of the platter, their red shells slathered in the sauce. The crabmeat was so sweet and, when mixed with the sweet-sour tang of the sauce, sent me to heaven. That truly delicious moment is one of my earliest and most influential food memories, so I just had to share this recipe.

SERVES 4

MUD CRAB

1 large mud crab, cleaned

1 medium brown or yellow onion, coarsely chopped

2 tbsp (22 g) finely chopped red chilies (any variety)

½ cup (120 ml) plus 1 tsp vegetable oil

½ tbsp (8 g) shrimp paste (belachan), crumbled

1 cup plus 2 tsp (250 ml) tomato puree

1 tbsp (15 g) tomato paste

1 cup (272 g) ketchup

¼ cup (60 ml) light soy sauce

2 tbsp (18 g) brown sugar

1 tbsp (15 ml) distilled white vinegar

½ tsp salt

¼ tsp cornstarch or potato starch mixed with ½ cup plus 1 tsp (125 ml) water

1 large egg, lightly beaten

SERVING SUGGESTIONS

Fresh cilantro leaves with stems

Steamed buns, rice or bread of choice

Remove the crab's top shell and set it aside, discarding any filters and grit. Cut the crab's body into quarters. Using the back of a heavy knife, mallet or pestle, crack the shells of the claws. Be careful not to hit the claws too hard or crack them too much. There should be only a few cracks so that the sauce can seep into the claws.

In a food processor, combine the onion and chilies. Process until they become a coarse puree.

Heat the oil in a large wok or large skillet over medium-high heat. Add the onion-chili puree and shrimp paste. Fry the mixture for 7 to 8 minutes, until the liquid has evaporated, the puree has deepened in color and some of the onion has started to brown.

Add the tomato puree, tomato paste, ketchup, soy sauce, brown sugar, vinegar and salt. Stir to combine the ingredients thoroughly. Stir-fry the mixture for 2 to 3 minutes, until the mixture is a uniform color.

Stir the cornstarch and water mixture well, making sure there are no lumps, and add it to the sauce. Stir thoroughly and allow the mixture to come to a boil.

Add the crab and the top shell to the sauce, tossing to coat everything. Reduce the heat to medium, cover the wok and simmer the mixture for 8 minutes, until the crab is bright orange-red and the flesh is firm and an opaque white.

Stir again to mix the crab and sauce well, then push the crab to one side of the wok. Add the egg to the sauce and immediately start stirring. Once the egg creates ribbons in the sauce, after about 30 seconds, stir the crab back into the mixture. Once the crab and sauce are thoroughly mixed, serve the crab on a large platter and garnish it with the cilantro. Serve the crab with steamed buns, rice or bread.

TIP: You can use other types of crab or even crayfish with this recipe.

NYONYA SPICY TAMARIND FISH CURRY
(ASSAM PEDAS)

I was on a family holiday in Malacca, Malaysia, when I discovered the explosion of flavors and aromas of *assam pedas ikan pari* (stingray) at a very busy Nyonya restaurant. Nyonya food comes from the Chinese immigrants that settled in Penang, Malacca and Singapore. The mix of Chinese, Malay and Portuguese flavors in Malacca is distinctive, intense and showcased beautifully in Nyonya cuisine. My cousins knew the owners of the restaurant, and they immediately greeted us with a giant silver bowl of the striking reddish-orange fish curry. The spicy, sour, oceanic flavor of this recipe is absolutely glorious.

SERVES 4

CURRY PASTE

3 cloves garlic

1 medium stalk lemongrass (white part only), thinly sliced

4 large red Asian shallots, coarsely chopped

10 dried red chilies (such as chile de árbols or guajillos), seeds removed

½ tbsp (8 g) shrimp paste (belachan), toasted

2 tbsp (30 ml) rice bran, canola or grapeseed oil

FISH

5 tbsp (75 ml) rice bran, canola or grapeseed oil

2 tsp (6 g) curry powder

1 tbsp (15 ml) tamarind puree

1 cup (240 ml) water

8 to 10 okra pods, stems removed (see Tip)

1 cup (160 g) coarsely chopped tomatoes

1 lb (450 g) bone-in firm fish (such as stingray, pomfret, kingfish, albacore, leatherjacket or cod), cut into large pieces

15 to 20 fresh Vietnamese mint leaves with stems

2 tsp (6 g) grated palm sugar or brown sugar

Salt, as needed

SERVING SUGGESTION

Steamed rice

To make the curry paste, combine the garlic, lemongrass, shallots, chilies, shrimp paste and oil in a blender. Blend until the ingredients are smooth.

To make the fish, heat the oil in a large wok or saucepan over medium heat. Add the curry paste and stir-fry it for 4 to 5 minutes, until the oil and paste are well combined, darkened in color and very fragrant.

Increase the heat to medium-high. Add the curry powder and tamarind puree. Stir-fry the mixture for 2 to 3 minutes, until the ingredients are well combined. Add the water, okra and tomatoes and bring the mixture to a boil.

Add the fish, Vietnamese mint, palm sugar and a generous pinch of salt. Stir to combine the curry, reduce the heat to low and simmer for 5 to 6 minutes, until the fish is completely opaque and easily separates from the bone.

Serve the fish curry with steamed rice.

TIP: You can add other vegetables. This dish works particularly well with eggplant, snake beans and cabbage.

MALAYSIAN FRIED RICE NOODLES
(CHAR KWAY TEOW)

I absolutely had to include the iconic Malaysian *char kway teow* in this book. This wok-fried noodle dish is deliciously decadent. Cooked in pork lard, char kway teow was originally a blue-collar dish—it was quick and cheap to whip up, and it gave laborers and fishermen the energy to go about their workday. Nowadays, it is one of the most commonly ordered and adored noodle dishes in the world. Fat is flavor, and the aroma and savoriness imparted by the pork lard is on par with crispy bacon or fried chicken to me.

SERVES 2

2 tbsp (30 ml) light soy sauce

1 tbsp (15 ml) dark soy sauce

½ tbsp (8 ml) oyster sauce

½ tbsp (8 ml) fish sauce

1 tsp sugar (optional)

½ tsp ground black pepper

1 lb (450 g) fresh flat rice noodles (banh pho)

3 tbsp (42 g) pork lard (see Tips)

2 cloves garlic, minced

1 large red Asian shallot, finely chopped

1 medium red serrano chili, thinly sliced or finely chopped (optional)

2 oz (56 g) lap cheong sausages (also known as Chinese sausages), thinly sliced

6 to 8 large fresh prawns, shelled and deveined

8 to 10 thin slices store-bought fish cake

1 large egg

1 cup (100 g) fresh bean sprouts

4 to 5 stems garlic chives (also known as Chinese chives), cut into 1-inch (2.5-cm) pieces

In a small bowl, mix together the light soy sauce, dark soy sauce, oyster sauce, fish sauce, sugar (if using) and black pepper. Set this mixture aside.

Carefully loosen the rice noodles with your hands. Set them aside.

Heat a large wok or skillet over high heat. Add the lard. Once the oil begins to smoke, add the garlic, shallot, chili (if using) and *lap cheong* sausages. Stir-fry the mixture with a spatula or wooden spoon for 20 to 30 seconds, then add the prawns and fish cake. Stir-fry the mixture for 30 to 40 seconds, then add the noodles and a drizzle of the soy sauce mixture. Stir-fry for another 1 to 2 minutes, gradually adding the rest of the soy sauce mixture and using a flipping motion to mix the ingredients together until everything is evenly coated in the soy sauce.

Create a well in the center of the wok and add the egg. Scramble the egg quickly for 10 seconds, until curds start to form. Move the other ingredients back into the center of the wok and stir-fry the mixture to combine everything.

Add the bean sprouts and garlic chives, tossing the wok for 10 to 15 seconds to ensure everything is thoroughly combined. Turn off the heat and serve the noodles immediately.

TIPS: If you don't care for pork lard, feel free to use a neutral oil such as rice bran, grapeseed or peanut oil in this recipe.

For the best results, make sure you fry the noodles on very high heat and that you fry a maximum of two servings at a time.

HAINANESE CHICKEN RICE

No trip to Singapore or Malaysia is complete without indulging in several plates of chicken rice. It is the perfect meal: succulent chicken paired with fragrant rice perfumed with pandan, bold sauces that elevate the chicken flavor and a savory chicken broth. The dish originated in Hainan, China, and was adapted from the Hainanese immigrants who moved to Malaysia and Singapore. It has become a piece of cultural identity. This must be one of the most contentious dishes among Malaysian and Singaporean families: "Who does it best? What method do you use to cook the chicken? What's in your sauce?" I've seen these questions rallied across the dinner table more vigorously than a tennis ball at the Australian Open. This recipe is my mum's version, and I'm willing to argue that it's the best.

SERVES 4 TO 5

CHICKEN RICE

1 (3½-lb [1.6-kg]) whole chicken

2 (1½-inch [4-cm]) pieces fresh ginger, unpeeled and lightly crushed

10 cloves garlic, peeled and lightly crushed, divided

8 spring onions, cut into 3-inch (7.5-cm) pieces

1 tbsp (15 g) salt

2 to 3 tsp (10 to 15 g) monosodium glutamate or 2 chicken stock cubes

4 tbsp (56 g) rendered chicken fat (see Tip)

3 cups (630 g) uncooked jasmine rice

2 fresh pandanus leaves, bruised and tied into knots, or 2 tsp (10 ml) pandan extract

1 to 2 tbsp (15 to 30 ml) toasted sesame oil

SERVING SUGGESTIONS

Thinly sliced cucumber

Fresh cilantro leaves with stems

Mum's "Everything" Sauce (page 115)

Spring Onion and Ginger Oil (page 119)

To make the chicken rice, remove the 2 pieces of chicken fat from inside the chicken cavity. These are usually attached to the entrance of the cavity and can be easily removed by pulling gently. Finely chop this fat if you are rendering your own chicken fat (see Tip).

Place the chicken, breast side up, in a large pot and fill it with cold water until it just covers the chicken. Add the ginger, 5 cloves of the garlic, spring onions, salt and monosodium glutamate. Bring the water to a boil over high heat, reduce the heat to low and simmer the chicken for 15 minutes. Turn off the heat and leave the chicken to poach in the soup for 20 minutes.

Carefully remove the chicken from the broth and use a meat hook to hang it, cavity-side down, over a large bowl. Allow the chicken to hang and rest for 10 minutes. Reserve the pot of chicken broth.

Heat the rendered chicken fat in a medium wok or skillet over medium-high heat. Add the remaining 5 cloves of garlic and rice. Stir-fry the rice for 1 to 2 minutes, until it is completely coated in the chicken fat. Transfer the rice and garlic to a rice cooker and add the pandanus leaves. Using the chicken broth instead of water, cook the rice according to the package instructions.

Once the rice is cooked and the chicken has cooled, remove the chicken from the meat hook. Add the liquid that drained into the bowl to the chicken broth in the pot and bring the broth to a boil over high heat. When the soup comes to a boil, turn off the heat immediately. Taste the broth for seasoning—add salt if needed or, if the broth is too salty, dilute it by adding more water.

Rub the chicken all over with the sesame oil. Cut it into pieces according to your preference and serve it on a bed of sliced cucumber.

Serve the chicken with the cilantro, rice, a bowl of the chicken broth, Mum's "Everything" Sauce and the Spring Onion and Ginger Oil on the side.

TIP: You can either purchase rendered chicken fat (*schmaltz*) or make your own by placing 4 ounces (112 g) of chopped raw chicken fat in a dry saucepan or small skillet and heating it over low heat. Cook the chicken fat for 20 to 30 minutes, until all the fat has rendered out and the solids shrink and become crispy and golden. You can add the solids and the rendered fat to the rice.

MALAYSIAN RICE AND HERB SALAD
(NASI ULAM)

I first had *nasi ulam* (a colorful herb and rice salad) on a childhood family vacation to Malacca, Malaysia, home of delicious and enticing Peranakan cuisine (which originated with descendants of Chinese immigrants to Malaysia and Singapore). When the herbaceous dish landed on the table, I was completely overwhelmed by the exciting colors: green from beans and leaves, gold from the turmeric rice and pops of pink from ginger torch flower. The refreshing sweetness of basil and mint, the citrusy lift of lemongrass and the savory, salty seafood flavor of the dried shrimp all adorned with a little spicy sambal belachan sauce was magical.

SERVES 4

½ cup (120 ml) rice bran, canola or grapeseed oil

½ cup (15 g) dried Asian anchovies (ikan bilis)

1 cup (80 g) dried shrimp (hebi)

2 medium stalks lemongrass (white parts only), thinly sliced

1 (2-inch [5-cm]) piece fresh galangal, coarsely chopped

Salt, as needed

4 cups (640 g) cooked rice, cooled

1⅓ cups (120 g) desiccated or shredded unsweetened coconut, toasted

1 cup (170 g) thinly sliced winged beans, snake beans or green beans

1 tbsp (9 g) ground turmeric

2 ginger torch flower buds, thinly sliced (optional)

4 large red Asian shallots, thinly sliced

Ground black pepper, as needed

8 fresh kaffir lime leaves, very thinly sliced

4 fresh betel leaves, very thinly sliced

12 fresh mint leaves

12 fresh Vietnamese mint leaves

12 fresh Thai basil leaves

2 medium red serrano chilies, thinly sliced

SERVING SUGGESTIONS
Sambal Belachan (page 120)

Lime wedges

Prawn crackers

Heat the oil in a small wok or skillet over medium-low heat. Add the dried anchovies and fry them for 8 to 10 minutes, or until they are deep brown and crispy. Turn off the heat, drain the anchovies and reserve the oil. Set the anchovies aside.

Using a mortar and pestle, pound the dried shrimp, lemongrass and galangal with a pinch of salt until a fine paste forms.

In a large bowl, mix together the shrimp paste, rice, coconut, winged beans, turmeric, ginger torch flowers (if using), shallots, a pinch of salt, a pinch of black pepper and 2 tablespoons (30 ml) of the reserved oil. Toss everything together well.

Add the kaffir lime leaves, betel leaves, mint leaves, Vietnamese mint leaves, Thai basil leaves and serrano chilies to the rice and mix well. Taste the mixture and adjust the seasoning with salt and black pepper.

Top the salad with the fried anchovies and serve it with the Sambal Belachan, lime wedges and prawn crackers on the side.

MALAYSIAN DRY MIXED NOODLES
(KAMPUA MEE)

Nothing is more perfect or satisfying than a plate of *kampua mee* and a cup of iced *kopi-o* (black coffee) for brunch at a bustling hawker center in Kuching, Malaysia. Rich and oily, kampua mee is a simple noodle dish that is packed with incredible flavor and quick to prepare. When my brother was last in Kuching, he ate two or three plates of these noodles every morning. He came back to Sydney 11 pounds (5 kg) heavier and happier. The mixture of both pork lard and shallot oil creates a luscious and savory oiliness. On the streets of Sarawak, Malaysia, it is typically served with *char siu*, a sweet roast pork that is great for mopping up some of the salty sauce. This recipe is based on my own family's recipe, and we prefer it with steamed pork belly for a slightly cleaner, less sweet flavor. The monosodium glutamate is optional in this recipe, but it certainly enriches the onion flavor.

SERVES 4 TO 5

SHALLOT OIL

1 cup (240 ml) rice bran, canola or grapeseed oil

8 large red Asian shallots, thinly sliced

NOODLES

3 tbsp (45 ml) dark soy sauce

1 tbsp (15 ml) light soy sauce

2 tbsp (28 g) pork lard

2 tbsp (30 ml) Sriracha chili sauce or chili sauce of choice

2 tsp (10 g) monosodium glutamate (optional)

2 tbsp (6 g) thinly sliced garlic chives

2 tbsp (6 g) thinly sliced spring onions

2 lbs (900 g) fresh egg noodles

SERVING SUGGESTIONS

Steamed or boiled pork belly, thinly sliced

4 to 5 fried eggs

To make the shallot oil, heat the oil in a small saucepan over medium heat. Add the shallots and stir. Reduce the heat to low and cook the shallots for 15 to 20 minutes, or until they are golden brown. Stir them gently every 2 to 3 minutes, watching them carefully since they can burn very quickly. (Resist the temptation to increase the heat if the shallots are taking a long time to start browning.)

Remove the shallots from the oil and transfer them to paper towels to drain. Reserve both the oil and the shallots (which will become crispy).

To make the noodles, combine the dark soy sauce, light soy sauce, 3 tablespoons (45 ml) of the shallot oil, pork lard, Sriracha chili sauce, monosodium glutamate (if using), garlic chives, spring onions and one-third of the crispy shallots in a large bowl. Set the mixture aside. (Any extra shallot oil can be kept in a jar in a cool, dark place for up to 4 weeks.)

Boil the egg noodles per the package instructions or to the desired doneness. Drain the noodles very well and add them to the bowl with the soy sauce mixture. Using tongs or chopsticks, stir and toss the noodles vigorously until everything is evenly combined and coated.

Serve the noodles topped with the remaining crispy shallots, pork belly and fried egg.

BELACHAN GREEN BEANS
WITH SHRIMP

This recipe is synonymous with my Malaysian family travels because of its pungent yet mouthwatering fragrance. It's one of those dishes my family and I know we're going to order at any sidewalk restaurant in Malaysia. It is consistently quick to the table and consistently delicious. There's a saltiness and complexity to the belachan and dried shrimp that is addictive. Even my brother, who loves meat far more than veggies, adores this dish with steamed rice. This recipe is a street food classic that is easily translated into an affordable, quick and tasty meal at home.

SERVES 2

1 tbsp (14 g) dried shrimp (hebi)

4 tbsp (60 ml) rice bran, canola or grapeseed oil

2 cloves garlic, thinly sliced

2 tsp (10 g) shrimp paste (belachan)

5 to 6 oz (140 to 168 g) green beans, trimmed (see Tips)

1 tbsp (15 ml) light soy sauce

Soak the dried shrimp in warm water for 10 to 15 minutes. Drain the shrimp well and pat them dry with paper towels.

Heat the oil in a medium wok or skillet over medium-high heat. When the oil starts to smoke, add the dried shrimp and garlic and stir-fry them for 1 to 2 minutes, or until the garlic begins to brown. Crumble the shrimp paste into the wok and stir-fry the mixture for 1 minute. Add the green beans and stir-fry them for 2 to 3 minutes. Add the soy sauce, tossing the green beans to coat them in the sauce, and stir-fry them for 1 to 2 minutes, until the green beans are evenly coated in the sauce.

Serve the green beans immediately. Do not let the green beans rest in the wok, as they will overcook.

TIPS: You can cut the green beans into 2-inch (5-cm) pieces if you prefer.

For a more decadent version of this dish, stir-fry the green beans in rendered pork lard or chicken fat. You can also replace the green beans with sugar snap peas, broccoli, asparagus or any hardy greens you enjoy.

CEREAL BUTTER PRAWNS

This is another iconic dish in Malaysian and Singaporean hawker centers. It uses Nestle's Nestum cereal, a flaky mixture of corn grits, wheat, rice and malt. Rolled oats are a suitable substitute if the cereal is unavailable to you. The prawn flavor works superbly with the creaminess of the butter and the toasty yet sweet nuttiness of the cereal. And the crispy curry leaves add an exciting boost of earthy flavor. Cereal butter prawns are one of the indulgences I allow myself to enjoy on trips back to Malaysia and Singapore or to prepare for family on occasions like Chinese New Year.

SERVES 4

7 to 9 large fresh prawns, heads and shells on

Rice bran, canola or grapeseed oil, as needed

1 cup (180 g) Nestle Nestum Original cereal or rolled oats

½ tsp salt

1 tbsp (12 g) sugar

2 tbsp (28 g) powdered whole milk

3 tbsp plus 2 tsp (55 g) salted butter

7 to 8 sprigs fresh curry leaves, stems removed

3 medium red serrano chilies or chilies of choice, thinly sliced

Using a sharp knife or kitchen scissors, cut the back of each prawn's shell, just far enough into the flesh to remove the vein but keeping the body shell intact. Cut off any long antennas or sharp spikes on each prawn's head, if desired.

Pat the prawns dry with paper towels. In a large pot, heat the oil to 350°F (177°C). Working in batches if necessary, add the prawns to the oil and fry them for 1 to 2 minutes, until they have become red, opaque and crispy on the outside. Transfer the prawns to paper towels to drain.

Combine the Nestum cereal, salt, sugar and powdered whole milk in a medium bowl. Melt the butter in a large skillet or wok over medium heat. Carefully add the curry leaves and serrano chilies and fry them for 30 to 40 seconds, until the curry leaves are crispy. (Use caution, as the curry leaves tend to cause spattering when placed in hot oil.)

Add the cereal mixture to the skillet. Stir-fry the mixture for 1 to 2 minutes, until it is golden brown and crispy. (If you are using oats, you may need to stir-fry the mixture a little longer for it to become crispy.)

Add the prawns to the mixture and stir again to mix well.

Serve the prawns on a platter.

HOKKIEN NOODLES

(HOKKIEN MEE)

This dish has a special place in my heart. It is the essential Malaysian street food experience. There are so many variations of this dish between states, cities and even neighborhoods. This is my mum's version, which is based on the version made in Kuala Lumpur with dark soy sauce. It is lip-smackingly saucy, the noodles are plump and the meat and veggies all add texture. It reminds me of casual family dinners at roadside hawkers. It is still a family favorite today, and I cook this once or twice a fortnight for my mum—it's probably the only dish that she'll admit I make as well as she does!

SERVES 5 TO 6

2 lbs (900 g) Hokkien noodles

7 oz (196 g) pork shoulder or Boston butt, thinly sliced or diced into bite-size pieces

1 tbsp (9 g) cornstarch

2 tbsp (30 ml) light soy sauce

3 tbsp (45 ml) rice bran, canola or grapeseed oil

2 large red Asian shallots or 1 brown or yellow onion, thinly sliced

4 cloves garlic, minced

8 pieces wood ear mushrooms (also known as black fungus), rehydrated in water for 10 minutes and large pieces cut smaller

6 tbsp (90 ml) dark soy sauce

4 cups (960 ml) boiling water

1 small bunch choy sum, cut into 1- to 2-inch (2.5- to 5-cm) pieces

1 cup (170 g) thinly sliced Chinese cabbage

SERVING SUGGESTIONS

Lemon wedges

Pickled chilies

Loosen the noodles from each other without tearing them.

Add the noodles to a dry large skillet or wok over high heat. Allow the noodles to scorch until some parts are blackened, then flip or stir the noodles around to blacken them further. This process can take 15 to 20 minutes and you should aim for about 40 to 50 percent of the noodles to be scorched.

In the meantime, thoroughly mix the pork with the cornstarch and light soy sauce in a medium bowl, making sure there are no dry bits of cornstarch.

Once the noodles have blackened, remove the noodles from the skillet and set them aside. Add the oil to the hot skillet, then add the shallots and garlic. Fry them for 1 to 2 minutes, until they are light gold. Add the pork and stir-fry it for 2 to 3 minutes, until the pork is brown.

Add the noodles to the pork mixture and stir-fry thoroughly to combine the ingredients. Add the mushrooms, dark soy sauce and boiling water to the noodles. Mix the ingredients well and cover the skillet with a lid. Cook the noodles for 10 to 15 minutes, undisturbed, until the noodles are very tender and have plumped up.

Add the choy sum and Chinese cabbage to the noodles. Stir-fry the mixture for 2 to 3 minutes. Serve the noodles with lemon wedges and pickled chilies.

GARLIC AND SOY SAUCE KANGKUNG

Garlic and soy *kangkung* is my go-to dish to cure homesickness. Kangkung is a leafy green vegetable with a hollow stem. It is also known as "morning glory" or "water spinach." Most commonly you'll find this served throughout Southeast Asia stir-fried with shrimp paste or fish sauce. I prefer the simpler version with garlic and soy sauce. There is something so comforting and wonderful about the crunchy yet tender straws of water spinach and the salty, umami richness of soy sauce and garlic.

The key to this dish is high heat and enough fat, so make sure you have all your ingredients ready to go before you start stir-frying—and don't be shy with the oil or lard.

SERVES 2

1 lb (450 g) kangkung (also known as water spinach or morning glory), cleaned

¼ cup (60 ml) rice bran, canola or grapeseed oil

4 cloves garlic, thinly sliced or minced

2 tbsp (30 ml) light soy sauce

1 tbsp (14 g) pork lard (optional; see Tip)

1 cup (160 g) steamed rice

Cut the kangkung into 3-inch (7.5-cm) pieces and set them aside next to the stove.

Heat the oil in a medium wok over high heat. When the oil is smoking intensely, add the garlic, immediately followed by the kangkung. Immediately toss and stir-fry the garlic and kangkung for 20 to 30 seconds. Add the soy sauce and pork lard (if using) and stir-fry the mixture for 30 to 40 seconds. The kangkung leaves should be wilted, the stems should be slightly crisp and the sauce should be coating everything.

Immediately transfer the kangkung and sauce to a serving platter. (Do not let it rest in the wok, as it will overcook.) Serve the kangkung with the steamed rice.

TIP: **If you would like to make this dish vegetarian, omit the pork lard.**

COCONUT PRAWNS

This recipe is inspired by the best parts of the creamy, coconutty seafood noodle soups that I grew up with. We had laksa and curry soup noodles from hawker centers regularly for dinner, and the prawns were my favorite part. I tend to always save one for the last precious mouthful. I've developed this recipe based on the joy that comes from biting into a tender yet springy prawn that is swimming in delicious coconut, kaffir lime and chili flavors. The broth is insanely delicious over rice!

SERVES 2

PRAWNS

12 large, shell-on fresh prawns

3 tbsp (45 ml) rice bran, canola or grapeseed oil

1 large red Asian shallot

2 cloves garlic

4 to 5 dried red chilies (such as chile de árbols or guajillos)

6 fresh kaffir lime leaves or traditional lime leaves, bruised

1 tsp coconut sugar or brown sugar

1½ cups (360 ml) water

¼ cup (19 g) unsweetened coconut flakes

1 tsp salt

1 cup (240 ml) full-fat coconut cream

SERVING SUGGESTIONS

Steamed rice or vermicelli noodles

Fresh cilantro leaves

Fresh mint leaves

Lime or kumquat wedges

Malaysian Turmeric Lace Pancakes (page 70)

Remove the heads, shells and veins from all the prawns, reserving the shells and heads. Use a toothpick or skewer to help you pull out the veins, or butterfly the backs of the prawns and remove the veins.

Heat the oil in a medium saucepan over medium-high heat. Add the prawns and fry them for 1 minute, just until they caramelize and become opaque on the outside. Remove the prawns from the saucepan and set them aside.

Add the shallot, garlic and chilies to the oil. Cook them for 2 to 3 minutes, until they begin to turn golden brown. Add the prawn heads and shells and stir-fry them for 2 to 3 minutes, until they become deep orange and crispy. Add the kaffir lime leaves, sugar and water. Reduce the heat to medium and bring the mixture to a simmer. Use a wooden spoon, ladle or potato masher to crush the prawn heads and shells to release more flavor. Cover the saucepan and simmer the broth for 10 to 15 minutes.

In the meantime, heat a small dry skillet over medium heat. Add the coconut flakes and toast them for 3 to 4 minutes, until they are golden. Set the coconut aside.

Remove the prawn broth from the heat and strain it into a medium saucepan. Discard the solids and return the broth to a simmer over medium heat. Add the salt, coconut cream and prawns. Simmer the mixture for 1 minute, or until the prawns are just slightly translucent in the center. Remove the saucepan from the heat.

Serve the prawns and broth with steamed rice or over vermicelli noodles. Top the prawns and broth with the toasted coconut flakes, cilantro leaves and mint leaves. Serve with the lime wedges and Malaysian Turmeric Lace Pancakes on the side.

MALAYSIAN BEEF RENDANG

Every time I have been served this exceptional dish, it was an act of love and celebration. In turn, I learned to make beef rendang and serve a pork version at my market stall, Pork Party, to honor and share that love. This is the kind of curry you can make in big batches by doubling or even tripling the recipe, so that you can portion it out to friends and family. The amazing fragrance and rich flavor come from the kaffir lime leaves and toasted coconut.

SERVES 4

PASTE

1 (1½-inch [4-cm]) piece fresh galangal or ginger

3 medium stalks lemongrass (white parts only)

4 large red Asian shallots

5 cloves garlic

1 to 2 tbsp (15 to 30 ml) rice bran, canola or grapeseed oil, if necessary

BEEF

1½ lbs (675 g) boneless beef short ribs or chuck steak, cut into large cubes

3 tbsp (24 g) all-purpose flour

½ cup (120 ml) rice bran, canola or grapeseed oil

2 (3-inch [7.5-cm]) cinnamon sticks

4 star anise pods

6 cardamom pods

8 fresh kaffir lime leaves, stems removed and thinly sliced

3 medium stalks lemongrass, bruised or lightly pounded

1 tsp hot chili powder

1 tbsp (9 g) brown sugar or grated palm sugar

1 cup (240 ml) water, plus more as needed

1 cup (240 ml) full-fat coconut cream

1½ tsp (8 g) salt

1 cup (90 g) desiccated coconut, toasted

SERVING SUGGESTIONS

Steamed rice

Malaysian Flatbread (page 69) or Malaysian Turmeric Lace Pancakes (page 70)

To make the paste, combine the galangal, lemongrass, shallots and garlic in a mortar. Pound the ingredients with a pestle until a finely textured paste forms. Alternatively, add the ingredients to a food processor and process until they form a paste. (You may need to add 1 or 2 tablespoons [15 to 30 ml] of oil to help the ingredients come together in the food processor.)

To make the beef, dust the beef cubes in the flour. Heat the oil in a large pot over medium-high heat until the oil starts smoking. Working in batches so as not to overcrowd the pot, add the beef to the pot, being careful not to disturb the searing pieces too much as you continue adding the remaining beef. Cook the beef for 2 minutes, flip it and fry it for 2 minutes, until the beef has a deep brown crust on both sides. Remove the beef cubes from the pot and set them aside.

Add the paste to the oil and stir-fry it for 3 to 4 minutes, until it is caramelized and fragrant. Add the cinnamon, star anise, cardamom, kaffir lime leaves and lemongrass. Stir-fry the mixture for 2 to 3 minutes, then add the chili powder, beef and brown sugar. Stir thoroughly to combine the ingredients well and stir-fry the mixture for another 2 to 3 minutes.

Add the water, coconut cream and salt to the beef. Reduce the heat to medium, stir the mixture well and bring it to a simmer. Cover the pot and cook the mixture for 15 to 20 minutes.

Add the coconut and stir the curry thoroughly. If the curry is dry, add 3 tablespoons (45 ml) of water at a time. Cover the pot again, reduce the heat to medium-low and simmer the curry for 60 to 90 minutes, or until the liquid has been completely absorbed and the meat is fork-tender.

Taste and adjust the seasonings. Serve the rendang with steamed rice and Malaysian Flatbread or Malaysian Turmeric Lace Pancakes.

TEOCHEW FISH BALL NOODLE SOUP

The incredibly tender, airy fish balls in this soup are a delight to eat, and the peppery flavor and light broth are invigorating. The addition of celery leaves is a unique touch from my mum's recipe. Starting out in my career as a lawyer, I worked some long nights. To reenergize and soothe me, Mum made this for breakfast on weekends. The moments I spent making the fish balls with her are precious. I hope that when you make this noodle soup, you feel and share the same love and care I received.

SERVES 4

FISH BALLS

8 oz (224 g) skinless tender whitefish fillets (such as saddletail snapper, haddock, cod or sole)

½ tsp salt

1½ tsp (3 g) ground black pepper

1 tbsp (9 g) cornstarch

1 tbsp (3 g) thinly sliced spring onion

1 large egg white

BROTH

6¼ cups (1.5 L) fish or chicken stock

1 tsp salt

1 tsp ground black pepper

7 oz (196 g) choy sum, washed and cut into 3-inch (7.5-cm) pieces

1 tbsp (3 g) finely chopped celery leaves

1 tbsp (3 g) thinly sliced spring onion

7 oz (196 g) vermicelli noodles, cooked

SERVING SUGGESTION

Chili Oil and Crispy Chili (page 116)

To make the fish balls, combine the fish, salt, black pepper, cornstarch, spring onion and egg white in a food processor. Process just until the ingredients come together and form a smooth paste. Using wet hands or 2 wet spoons, form fish balls that are about 1 to 1½ inches (2.5 to 4 cm) in diameter. Set the fish balls aside.

To make the broth, combine the stock, salt and black pepper in a large pot over high heat. Bring the broth to a boil. Reduce the heat to medium. Add the choy sum, celery leaves, spring onion and fish balls to the soup and simmer it for 3 to 4 minutes, until the fish balls are all floating at the surface and are completely opaque and white. The fish should be springy to the touch. Turn off the heat.

Divide the cooked vermicelli noodles among 4 soup bowls. Top the noodles with the soup. Serve the soup immediately with a drizzle of the Chili Oil and Crispy Chili.

TIP: You could form these fish balls the day before. Simply keep them, covered, in the refrigerator.

PROPER PORK LARB

Pork larb is one of the first Thai dishes I learned to make after falling in love with its perfect balance of flavors. It was a refreshing discovery after the richness and sweetness of the less-than-authentic Thai dishes I had experienced in Sydney. This larb has a hint of sweetness that draws out the savory nuttiness of the glutinous rice and pork. That's the real magic behind larb: An authentic larb will have toasted glutinous rice in it, and most recipes on the internet simply do not include it. The glutinous rice adds a nutty roundness to the dish that transforms the recipe from a stir-fry of ground meat and herbs to a cleverly constructed dish filled with flavor, texture and harmony.

SERVES 3 TO 4

PORK LARB

3 tbsp (39 g) uncooked Thai glutinous rice

4 to 5 tbsp (60 to 75 ml) rice bran, canola or grapeseed oil

3 large red Asian shallots, thinly sliced

3 cloves garlic, thinly sliced

1 lb (450 g) ground pork (see Tips)

1 tbsp (9 g) red pepper flakes

1 tsp sugar

1 tbsp (15 ml) fish sauce

Juice of 2 medium limes

3 spring onions, thinly sliced

20 fresh Thai basil leaves (see Tips), divided

15 fresh mint leaves, divided

SERVING SUGGESTIONS

Pork crackling

Lime wedges

Glutinous or steamed rice

To make the pork larb, toast the Thai glutinous rice in a dry, medium skillet over medium heat for 15 to 20 minutes, until it is a deep gold color. Stir the rice frequently to avoid burning.

Allow the rice to cool, then grind the rice into a powder using a mortar and pestle, food processor or spice grinder. Set the rice powder aside.

Heat the oil in a large wok or frying pan over medium-high heat until the oil starts smoking. Add the shallots and garlic and fry them for 1 to 2 minutes, until they begin to caramelize. Crumble in the ground pork and stir-fry it for 5 to 6 minutes, or until the pork is brown and cooked through.

Add the red pepper flakes, sugar and fish sauce to the pork mixture. Stir-fry the mixture for 1 to 2 minutes, then add the lime juice, rice powder and spring onions. Mix the ingredients well and turn off the heat. Allow the larb to cool for 3 to 4 minutes, then add 10 of the basil leaves and 7 of the mint leaves. Stir the larb to combine the ingredients. Top the larb with the remaining 10 basil leaves, remaining 8 mint leaves, pork crackling, lime wedges and glutinous or steamed rice.

TIPS: You can trade the ground pork for ground chicken, veal or beef.

You can use any type of basil you like in this recipe.

The toasted rice powder can be kept in an air-tight container, out of the fridge, for 2 to 3 weeks.

KHMER BEEF CURRY

Khmer food was an extraordinary challenge and surprise to my teenage eyes. There were ingredients I could not recognize and flavors I had never experienced. I kept questioning whether I was eating a version of Thai food or Vietnamese food. My naivety was broken when I tasted Khmer beef curry. I fell in love with it, and I immediately understood the dish to be distinctly Khmer. The nutty, toasted flavor of peanuts and round, soulful flavors of onions, shallots, lemongrass, cardamom and cilantro was a perfect marriage with the tender beef. As I was surrounded by French architecture and fringed by the mighty Mekong River in Kampong Cham, Cambodia, it made total sense for sixteen-year-old me to eat hunks of warm French baguette dipped into this curry for breakfast every day for ten days straight.

SERVES 6

MARINATED BEEF

2 lbs (900 g) beef chuck, cut into 1- to 1½-inch (2.5- to 4-cm) cubes

1 tsp salt

1 tsp ground black pepper

3 cloves garlic, minced

2 tsp (2 g) grated fresh ginger

Juice of ½ medium lime

CURRY PASTE

3 tbsp (24 g) finely ground peanuts

2 tbsp (18 g) curry powder

1 tsp shrimp paste (belachan)

2 tsp (6 g) paprika

½ tbsp (2 g) grated fresh ginger

1 (1-inch [2.5-cm]) piece fresh galangal, crushed

2 fresh cilantro roots

4 cloves garlic, crushed

1 large onion, diced

1 tbsp (15 ml) rice bran, canola or grapeseed oil

CURRY

3 tbsp (45 ml) rice bran, canola or grapeseed oil

2 dried bay leaves

4 cardamom pods

4 cloves

1 (3- to 4-inch [7.5- to 10-cm]) cinnamon stick

4 medium stalks lemongrass (white parts only), thinly sliced

4 large red Asian shallots, thinly sliced

1¼ cups (300 ml) full-fat coconut milk

6 fresh kaffir lime leaves or traditional lime leaves, bruised

1 tsp ground black pepper

1½ tsp (8 g) salt

SERVING SUGGESTIONS

Baguettes or steamed rice

To make the marinated beef, combine the beef, salt, black pepper, garlic, ginger and lime juice in a large bowl. Mix the ingredients together thoroughly and put the beef in the refrigerator to marinate for at least 30 minutes.

To make the curry paste, combine the peanuts, curry powder, shrimp paste, paprika, ginger, galangal, cilantro roots, garlic and onion in a mortar. Pound the ingredients with a pestle until a smooth paste forms. Add the oil and mix until the curry paste is well combined. Alternatively, combine the ingredients in a food processor and process until a smooth paste forms.

To make the curry, heat the oil in a large saucepan over high heat until the oil starts to smoke. Working in batches so as to not overcrowd the saucepan, add the marinated beef and fry it for 1 to 2 minutes on each side, or until it is brown all over. Remove the beef from the saucepan and set the beef aside. Reduce the heat to medium-high.

Add the bay leaves, cardamom pods, cloves, cinnamon stick, lemongrass and shallots to the saucepan and stir-fry the spices and shallots for 2 to 3 minutes, until they are fragrant and the shallots begin to turn golden brown. Add the curry paste and stir-fry it for 5 to 6 minutes, until it has dried considerably and become dark in color.

Add the beef, coconut milk, kaffir lime leaves, black pepper and salt to the saucepan. Mix the curry well and bring it to a boil. Reduce the heat to low, cover the saucepan and simmer the curry for 1 hour, or until the beef is fork-tender.

Serve the curry with the baguettes or steamed rice.

VIETNAMESE BEEF STEW

The first time I had this hearty dish, I was served by a gentle-faced, warm woman with a few teeth missing. She barely spoke English, but her body language and her cooking exuded love and hospitality. The stew was orange-brown and the gravy was on the thinner side and surrounded chunks of beef and bright carrots. The aroma of star anise, cloves and tomatoes wafted through the air. The stew was pure joy, with all the charm of warm spices and the French-influenced richness of tomatoes and crusty bread.

SERVES 4

MARINATED BEEF

2.6 lb (1.2 kg) beef shin, chuck steak or brisket, cut into roughly 1½-inch (4-cm) cubes

1 medium stalk lemongrass (white part only), bruised and thinly sliced

2 tbsp (30 ml) fish sauce

1 tbsp (9 g) brown sugar

2 tsp (6 g) five-spice powder

1 tbsp (15 ml) rice bran, canola or grapeseed oil

STEW

⅓ cup (80 ml) rice bran, canola or grapeseed oil

3 tbsp (24 g) all-purpose flour

3 star anise pods

1 (3-inch [7.5-cm]) cinnamon stick

3 large red Asian shallots or 1 large brown or white onion, finely chopped

3 cloves garlic, finely chopped

1 (1-inch [2.5-cm]) piece fresh ginger, unpeeled and thinly sliced

4 tbsp (60 g) tomato paste

1 tbsp (15 ml) fish sauce

1 tsp salt

1 tsp ground black pepper

3 to 4 cups (720 to 960 ml) water

2 large carrots, cut into bite-size pieces

SERVING SUGGESTIONS

Fresh cilantro leaves

Baguettes or steamed rice

To make the marinated beef, combine the beef, lemongrass, fish sauce, brown sugar, five-spice powder and oil in a large bowl. Mix thoroughly to ensure the beef is coated in the marinade. Marinate the beef for 20 to 30 minutes.

To make the stew, heat the oil in a tall pot over medium-high heat until it starts to smoke. While the oil is heating, remove the beef from the marinade and dust the beef with the flour.

Once the oil begins to smoke, add the beef to the pot in batches and sear each side for 1 to 2 minutes, until the beef is brown all over. Remove the beef from the pot and set it aside.

In the same pot, combine the star anise, cinnamon, shallots, garlic and ginger. Stir-fry for 2 to 3 minutes, until the shallots begin to caramelize and the spices are fragrant. Add the beef and any resting juices to the pot. Add the tomato paste, fish sauce, salt and black pepper. Stir-fry the mixture for 3 to 4 minutes, until the ingredients are thoroughly combined and the tomato paste has been incorporated.

Add the water to the pot and bring the stew to a boil. Reduce the heat to low and simmer the stew for 1½ hours. Add the carrots and simmer the stew for 30 minutes, or until the beef is fork-tender.

Taste the stew and add additional fish sauce or salt if needed. If the stew is too salty, add a little water.

Serve the stew with the cilantro and baguettes or steamed rice.

SAMBAL EGGPLANT

Spicy, sweet and deliciously silky, sambal eggplant is an iconic dish of Malaysia and Singapore and one of the first dishes I learned to cook with my Sambal Belachan (page 120). The eggplant is stir-fried over extremely high heat and then simmered in the sauce, which gives it the most amazing texture as it soaks up all the flavors. Sambal Eggplant is a testament to some of the best home-style cooking in Southeast Asia: simple yet powerful in flavor. Piled into a bowl of steaming white rice, this recipe is so moreish!

SERVES 2

SAMBAL EGGPLANT

3 tbsp (45 ml) rice bran, canola or grapeseed oil

1 (6-oz [168-g]) eggplant, cut into large chunks (see Tip)

1 tbsp (5 g) dried shrimp (hebi), lightly crushed

2 tbsp (30 g) Sambal Belachan (page 120), or store-bought

¼ cup (60 ml) water

Salt, as needed (optional)

SERVING SUGGESTIONS

Fresh cilantro leaves with stems

Steamed rice

To make the sambal eggplant, heat the oil in a medium wok or skillet over high heat. Once the oil begins to smoke, add the eggplant and dried shrimp and stir-fry them for 3 to 4 minutes, until the eggplant is golden brown.

Add the Sambal Belachan and toss to thoroughly coat the eggplant. Add the water and stir the eggplant again. Reduce the heat to medium-low. Simmer the eggplant for 2 to 3 minutes, until it has softened. Taste the eggplant and season it with the salt if needed.

Serve the eggplant with the cilantro and steamed rice.

TIP: I recommend globe, Italian or Indian eggplants.

STREET FOOD SAUCES

Every Southeast Asian country has some combination of sweet, savory and funky flavors in their sauces, and there is a lot of crossover among them. I've written a small selection of recipes for sauces that are the most versatile and easy to make; sauces that you can rely on to make the most amazing home-cooked meals and street food–inspired dishes. In this chapter alone, the flavor possibilities are endless: Make a mean marinade with Sambal Belachan (page 120), or create a flavorful oil base for roasts with my Chili Oil and Crispy Chili (page 116). Step up your stir-fries, create unforgettable curries, season steaks, whip up wickedly delicious salads and create soulful soups that satisfy with the help of the flavor bombs in this chapter.

MUM'S "EVERYTHING" SAUCE

On the streets of Southeast Asia, the official name for this type of sauce is *sambal oelek*: a vinegary, hot, bright red chili sauce that pairs exceptionally well with seafood. Don't limit yourself, though—this sauce goes with everything, hence its name. Mum never used a cookbook when she learned to cook in her late teens and early twenties as a brave new immigrant to Australia. Everything was made by taste and feel. She'll tell you there were a lot of disasters, but the one thing that has always been tried and true is her chili sauce. In the words of my mum, "Put it on everything!" This is a magical, raw, garlicky sauce that is potent in flavor.

MAKES 1 TO 1½ CUPS (240 TO 360 ML)

6 large red serrano chilies, coarsely chopped

2 small red bird's eye chilies, coarsely chopped

4 cloves garlic, coarsely chopped

1 (½-inch [13-mm]) piece fresh ginger, coarsely chopped

1 cup (240 ml) distilled white vinegar

Salt, as needed

In a small food processor, combine the serrano chilies, bird's eye chilies, garlic and ginger. Process the ingredients into a fine mixture with no large chunks of chilies or garlic remaining. (Alternatively, you can use a mortar and pestle for this, but the texture will be more like a puree.)

Transfer the chili mixture to a small bowl. Add the vinegar and season the sauce with the salt. Mix the sauce well before serving.

TIP: This sauce should be stored in the fridge in an airtight container and will keep up to 4 weeks.

CHILI OIL AND CRISPY CHILI

The combination of garlic, cloves, cinnamon and star anise is tremendous. In Southeast Asian cooking, it's often this combination that brings a depth of fragrance and flavor to soups, stocks and sauces. In this recipe, the combo is added to ginger, red pepper flakes and oil, which complete the harmonious group. The oil enhances flavor and adds a wonderful silkiness to dishes. Use this oil in your noodle soups (like my Teochew Fish Ball Noodle Soup on page 103), with dumplings, on poached chicken and on steamed fish. I'll bet this chili oil becomes a pantry staple for you!

MAKES 2½ CUPS (600 ML)

4 small red Asian shallots, thinly sliced

2 heads garlic, cloves peeled and thinly sliced

5 cloves

3 (3-inch [7.5-cm]) cinnamon sticks

6 star anise pods

2 (1½-inch [4-cm]) pieces fresh ginger, crushed

2½ cups (600 ml) rice bran, canola or grapeseed oil

¾ cup (108 g) red pepper flakes

2 tsp (10 g) salt

1 tsp sugar

2 tsp (10 g) monosodium glutamate (optional)

In a small saucepan over medium heat, combine the shallots, garlic, cloves, cinnamon sticks, star anise, ginger and oil. When the oil starts to bubble around the ingredients, reduce the heat to low. Simmer the oil for 40 to 45 minutes, or until the shallots and garlic have deeply browned, stirring occasionally. Keep an eye on the shallots and garlic as they can burn quite quickly after they have browned.

In the meantime, combine the red pepper flakes, salt, sugar and monosodium glutamate (if using) in a small heatproof bowl.

Remove the cinnamon sticks, cloves, star anise and ginger from the saucepan and discard them. Carefully pour the hot oil over the red pepper flakes mixture and mix well. Leave the oil to cool to room temperature, stirring occasionally.

Serve the Chili Oil and Crispy Chili with grilled meats, fried rice, noodles or on eggs.

TIP: The chili oil can be stored in a jar or airtight container in a cool, dark place for up to 4 weeks.

SPRING ONION AND GINGER OIL

This classic Chinese-style sauce is delicious over poached chicken or steamed fish. The intensely flavored, lip-smacking oil is perfect to pair with lighter dishes like Hainanese Chicken Rice (page 84) because it adds savoriness and richness. This sauce has been a part of my family dinner table for as long as I can remember. My family's recipe is simple yet so flavorful. Singapore is the only place I've found similar sauces that come close to the deliciousness of my family's!

MAKES 1 CUP (240 ML)

1 cup (240 ml) rice bran, canola or grapeseed oil or 1 cup (224 g) rendered chicken fat

1 tbsp (3 g) grated fresh ginger

2 cloves garlic, grated

1 tsp coarse salt

½ tsp monosodium glutamate

6 spring onions, thinly sliced

Heat the oil in a small saucepan over medium-high heat until it starts to smoke. Turn off the heat and add the ginger, garlic, salt, monosodium glutamate and spring onions to the saucepan. Stir thoroughly and leave the oil to steep and cool for 10 to 15 minutes.

TIP: This sauce can be stored in a sealed container in the fridge for up to 2 weeks. Let it come to room temperature before serving.

SAMBAL BELACHAN

There's nothing like walking through a bustling night market on a balmy night in Kuala Lumpur, Malaysia, and taking in all the delicious sights and sounds. The experience is made even more tempting by the incredible smells of grilled meat, heady stocks and fried treats. The aroma that rises above all of them is *belachan*. This pungent, fermented shrimp paste is iconic to Southeast Asian cooking. Used the right way, belachan is pure umami—the definition of tasty. You will not find a Malaysian food cart, *kopitiam* or restaurant without Sambal Belachan. It's a piece of the Malaysian national identity and finds its way into *laksa*, fried noodles, *nasi goreng*, dipping sauces, stir-fries and even fried eggs! A little bit goes a long way, and I highly recommend toasting this powerful paste outside or with all your doors and windows open—belachan is extremely tasty but extremely pungent. If you're brave enough to give this paste a try, it will change your life in the tastiest way.

MAKES APPROXIMATELY ½ CUP (120 G)

1 tbsp plus 1 tsp (20 g) shrimp paste (belachan)

5 to 6 (98 g) red serrano chilies, coarsely chopped

4 cloves garlic

1 tsp sugar

3 tbsp (45 ml) fresh calamansi lime juice or traditional lime juice

⅓ cup (80 ml) rice bran, canola or grapeseed oil

Salt, as needed

In a dry, small skillet over medium-low heat, toast the belachan for 6 to 8 minutes. The belachan will become very aromatic, dry and crumbly, and the color may become slightly lighter.

Transfer the belachan to a mortar. Add the chilies and garlic and use a pestle to pound the ingredients into a fine paste. Add the sugar and calamansi lime juice and combine well. Slowly add the oil, stirring as you go to mix everything well. Taste the Sambal Belachan and season it with the salt. Alternatively, combine the belachan, chilies, garlic, sugar, calamansi lime juice, oil and salt in a blender or food processor. Blend the ingredients until they are smooth.

TIP: Store the Sambal Belachan in a clean, dry jar in the refrigerator for 2 weeks. The Sambal Belachan can be frozen for up to 3 months.

INDONESIAN TOMATO SAMBAL

This sweet, tangy, umami bomb of a sauce is divine with fried food. One of my most delicious food memories was while I was working in Kuala Lumpur, Malaysia, and my mother was visiting. One weekend, we bought a greasy bag of *ayam goreng* (fried chicken) from the food court around the corner from the hotel. We sat in the air-conditioning sipping from ice-cold young coconuts and slathering this tomato sambal all over the deliciously crispy chicken. It was a special moment of bonding with Mum. Try this sambal with my Malaysian Barbecued Chicken with Coconut and Turmeric (page 19).

MAKES ½ CUP (120 G)

TOMATO SAMBAL

6 medium red serrano chilies

3 large red Asian shallots

5 cloves garlic

3 large tomatoes, coarsely chopped

3 candlenuts or macadamia nuts

6 tbsp (90 ml) rice bran, canola or grapeseed oil

1 tsp shrimp paste (belachan), crumbled

Salt, as needed

SERVING SUGGESTION

Lime wedges

In a food processor or blender, combine the serrano chilies, shallots, garlic, tomatoes and candlenuts. Process until the ingredients form a coarse or chunky salsa consistency.

Heat the oil in a medium wok or skillet over medium heat. Add the tomato mixture and belachan and stir-fry it for 6 to 7 minutes, or until the mixture has reduced by half and the oil separates. Season the sambal with the salt.

Serve the sambal with lime wedges to squeeze over the top. This sambal works perfectly with barbecued seafood and meat or Grilled Sticky Rice with Dried Shrimp and Coconut (page 39).

COCONUT SAMBAL

Sri Lankan coconut sambal is one of my favorite side dishes to eat with curries and roti. However, when I discovered a Malaysian version during my recent travels, I was blown away by how familiar yet distinctively Malaysian the sambal was. The same sweet coconut, fiery chilies and pungent onion flavors were all there. But the use of dried shrimp instead of Maldivian fish created a different savory funk and that made me crave the sambal more and more. This sauce is epic paired with my Grilled Spicy Pineapple (page 36).

MAKES 1 CUP (240 G)

3 to 4 tbsp (15 to 20 g) dried shrimp (hebi), soaked in warm water for 10 to 15 minutes (optional; see Tips)

1 cup (90 g) shredded fresh coconut or rehydrated desiccated coconut (see Tips)

2 large red Asian shallots, minced

2 cloves garlic, minced

2 tsp (6 g) hot chili powder

Juice of ½ medium lime

Pinch of salt

Ground white pepper, as needed

If you are using the dried shrimp, pound the shrimp using a mortar and pestle or finely chop it.

In a small bowl, combine the shrimp, coconut, shallots, garlic and chili powder. Stir the mixture thoroughly, until the chili powder is incorporated. (I recommend using your fingers to massage and squeeze the sambal together to achieve an even mixture.)

Add the lime juice, salt and white pepper and mix again. Adjust the seasoning to your preference.

Serve the coconut sambal with Malaysian Flatbread (page 69), Malaysian Turmeric Lace Pancakes (page 70) or sticky rice.

TIPS: If you would prefer to make this sambal vegan, omit the dried shrimp.

Unsweetened desiccated coconut can be rehydrated by mixing ¾ cup (70 g) desiccated coconut with 3 to 4 tablespoons (45 to 60 ml) full-fat coconut milk or water. Let the coconut rehydrate for 10 minutes, stirring occasionally.

VIETNAMESE SPICY DIPPING SAUCE
(NUOC CHAM)

This Vietnamese sauce is a staple. It is sweet, sour, salty and simple. You can't escape the heady aromas of fish sauce and garlic in Vietnam, and they are captured perfectly in the essence of *nuoc cham*. Vietnamese people have a talent for creating mouthwatering flavor by using fish sauce as a flavor enhancer. This sauce is the perfect accompaniment to my Vietnamese Crispy Spring Rolls (page 50) and Laotian Meatballs (page 49).

MAKES ⅓ CUP (80 ML)

1 tbsp (12 g) sugar

3 tbsp (45 ml) warm water

1 tbsp (15 ml) fresh lime juice

1 tbsp (15 ml) fish sauce

1 small bird's eye chili, thinly sliced

1 clove garlic, thinly sliced

In a small bowl, dissolve the sugar in the warm water. Mix in the lime juice, fish sauce, chili and garlic.

Store the sauce in the refrigerator for up to 4 weeks.

TIPS: This recipe can be easily adjusted to your taste. Increase or decrease the sugar, lime, fish sauce and chili to your desired sweetness, sourness, saltiness or spiciness.

Nuoc cham can be made in large batches. Store any leftovers in the refrigerator for up to 4 weeks.

THAI SWEET CHILI SAUCE
(NAM JIM GAI)

This sauce is named for its use with grilled or fried chicken. *Gai* means "chicken" in Thai. But honestly, this sauce works with everything from barbecued chicken to grilled prawns to grilled cheese sandwiches. I've added cilantro roots and stems to this recipe for an amazing aroma and herbaceous flavor.

MAKES ½ CUP (120 ML)

4 large red or green serrano chilies (see Tips)

2 cloves garlic

1 cilantro root with stems

3 tbsp (45 ml) rice bran, canola or grapeseed oil (see Tips)

½ cup (120 ml) distilled white vinegar or vinegar of choice

1 tbsp (15 ml) fish sauce

1 tbsp (12 g) sugar

Salt, as needed

In a food processor or blender, combine the serrano chilies, garlic and cilantro root with stems. Process to form a coarse paste. Alternatively, use a knife to finely chop all the ingredients into a coarse paste.

Heat the oil in a small saucepan over medium heat. Add the chili paste and stir it for 3 to 4 minutes, until the ingredients have softened.

Add the vinegar, fish sauce and sugar and stir thoroughly to combine. Reduce the heat to low and cook the sauce for 5 to 15 minutes, stirring occasionally, until most of the vinegar has been absorbed and the consistency is jammy and chunky.

Taste the sauce and season it with the salt to your preference.

Allow the sauce to cool completely before putting it in a clean, dry container.

Tips: The sauce can be stored in the refrigerator for up to 3 weeks.

If you prefer a milder sauce, remove the seeds from the serrano chilies prior to processing them with the other ingredients.

When you are processing the paste, adding 1 tablespoon (15 ml) of oil can help bring the ingredients together.

CREAMY MALAYSIAN PEANUT SAUCE

Satay and peanut sauce is one of the most iconic duos of Southeast Asian cuisine. I remember licking the bowl clean after a big dinner of satay skewers at the local grills in Kuala Lumpur and Kuching, Malaysia. This nutty, creamy, sweet and salty sauce is the perfect accompaniment to grilled meats and vegetables. You could even add it to salads and stir-fries. There's just something so satisfying and joyful about this recipe.

MAKES 1 CUP (240 ML)

1 cup (150 g) salted peanuts, finely ground

1 tbsp (9 g) curry powder

1 tbsp (15 g) tamarind paste or 1 tbsp (10 g) tamarind pulp mixed with 1 tbsp (15 ml) water

1½ tbsp (14 g) brown sugar

½ cup (120 ml) water

Heat a small dry saucepan over low heat. Add the peanuts and toast them for 4 to 5 minutes, stirring occasionally to avoid burning. Add the curry powder and stir the peanuts and curry powder together for 30 to 40 seconds.

Add the tamarind paste and brown sugar and mix thoroughly. Add the water and stir to combine. Bring the mixture to a simmer and cook it for 5 to 10 minutes, or until it has reduced to your desired consistency.

TIPS: You can adjust the chunkiness of the sauce by adjusting how finely ground your peanuts are. The coarser the grind, the more crunchy and textural the sauce will be.

This sauce can be kept in an airtight container in the fridge for up to 1 week.

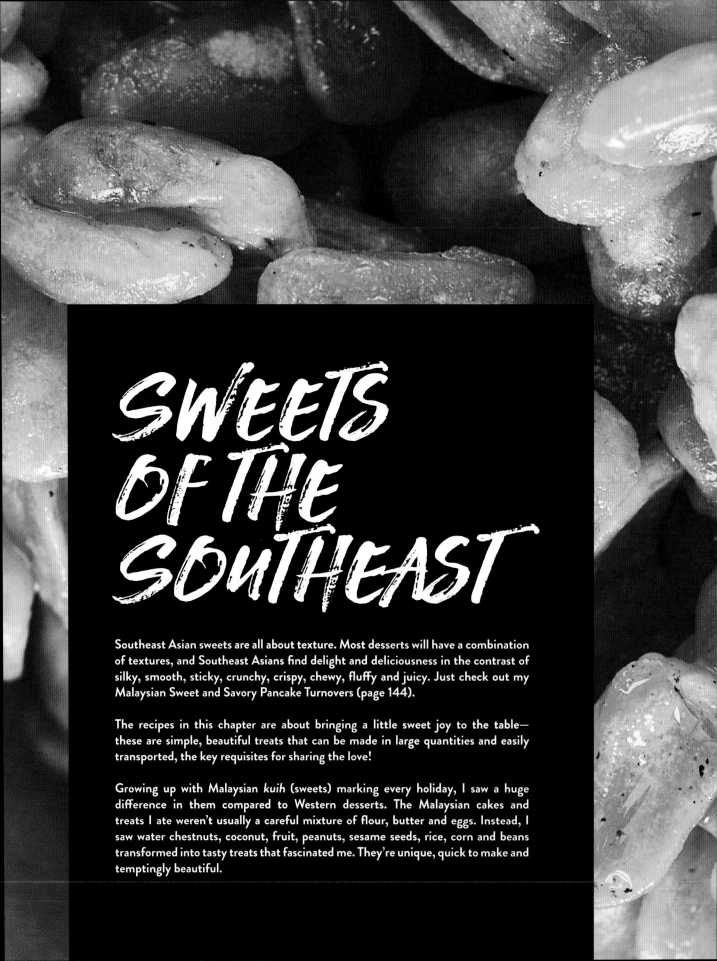

SWEETS OF THE SOUTHEAST

Southeast Asian sweets are all about texture. Most desserts will have a combination of textures, and Southeast Asians find delight and deliciousness in the contrast of silky, smooth, sticky, crunchy, crispy, chewy, fluffy and juicy. Just check out my Malaysian Sweet and Savory Pancake Turnovers (page 144).

The recipes in this chapter are about bringing a little sweet joy to the table— these are simple, beautiful treats that can be made in large quantities and easily transported, the key requisites for sharing the love!

Growing up with Malaysian *kuih* (sweets) marking every holiday, I saw a huge difference in them compared to Western desserts. The Malaysian cakes and treats I ate weren't usually a careful mixture of flour, butter and eggs. Instead, I saw water chestnuts, coconut, fruit, peanuts, sesame seeds, rice, corn and beans transformed into tasty treats that fascinated me. They're unique, quick to make and temptingly beautiful.

COCONUT SAGO PUDDING
WITH PALM SUGAR CARAMEL

This dessert is made with sticky sago pearls that are coated in creamy coconut milk and topped with a rich, sweet palm sugar caramel. *Sago*, or tapioca, is hugely popular in desserts throughout Malaysia, Singapore and Thailand. It is a textural delight: chewy-centered pearls enrobed in silky coconut milk. The pearls themselves don't have a flavor, so the addition of syrups, caramels or creams is necessary. The sago pearls are a wonderful base on which to build any combination of sweet flavors. Palm sugar is a perfect pairing with rich coconut sago pudding—it has a warm aroma, like a cross between vanilla and coconut. This recipe can be made one or two days in advance.

SERVES 3 TO 4

PUDDING

½ cup (76 g) tapioca pearls

3 cups (720 ml) water, divided, plus more as needed

¼ tsp salt

1 (13½-oz [405-ml]) can full-fat coconut milk

CARAMEL

¼ cup (56 g) unsalted butter

1⅓ cups plus 1 tbsp (200 g) palm sugar, grated, or dark brown sugar

¼ cup (60 ml) cream

¼ tsp salt

To make the pudding, soak the tapioca in 1 cup (240 ml) of the water for 15 minutes. Drain the tapioca and transfer it to a medium saucepan. Add the remaining 2 cups (480 ml) of water and salt. Bring the tapioca to a boil over medium-high heat.

Reduce the heat to medium-low and simmer the tapioca for 10 minutes, stirring occasionally. If the tapioca begins to spit or the water evaporates too fast, add water, 1 tablespoon (15 ml) at a time, and reduce the heat to low.

Turn off the heat and cover the saucepan with a lid. Let the tapioca steam, undisturbed, for 5 to 10 minutes, or until it is completely cooked through and translucent. Transfer the cooked tapioca to a medium bowl or container and chill it in the refrigerator, covered, for at least 1 hour.

Prepare the caramel just before serving the pudding. Melt the butter in a small saucepan over medium heat and cook it for 3 to 4 minutes, until it becomes a dark, nutty brown. Add the palm sugar and stir to dissolve it in the butter. Stir the mixture occasionally and cook it for 4 to 5 minutes, until the butter and sugar thicken. Add the cream and salt and stir the mixture until it is uniform in color. Allow the caramel to cool to room temperature.

To serve, place about ½ cup (130 g) of tapioca in each serving bowl or glass. Mix each portion with about ¼ cup (60 ml) of coconut milk. Allow the tapioca mixture to settle in each bowl or glass, then gently pour some of the caramel over the top.

TIP: You can prepare the tapioca a day ahead of serving and then prepare the caramel just before you want to serve.

BANANA FRITTERS
(PISANG GORENG)

There's a small food cart in the Brickfields suburb of Kuala Lumpur, Malaysia, right in front of the Shangri-La Restoran (no association to the hotels). The cart is run by a young but stern gentleman who serves three different things: fried taro, fried curry puffs and *pisang goreng* (fried banana fritters). He stands behind the roaring jet flame of a gas burner with a giant wok of bubbling oil sitting above it. With one hand, he batters the bananas and slips them into the oil. With the other hand, he skillfully flips the goods as soon as they are crunchy and golden brown. The pisang goreng are sweet like caramel and soft like warm custard on the inside. The banana fritters were a fantastic snack to munch on as you wandered down the road to explore Little India.

SERVES 4 TO 6

½ cup (60 g) all-purpose flour

¼ cup (38 g) rice flour

1 tsp baking powder

¼ tsp salt

1 cup plus 2 tsp (250 ml) water

1 large egg, beaten

Rice bran, canola or grapeseed oil, as needed

6 large ripe bananas, peeled and cut into halves or thirds

In a medium bowl, mix together the all-purpose flour, rice flour, baking powder and salt until they are well combined. Whisk in the water and egg until the batter is smooth. The batter should have the consistency of pancake batter, and it should run off a spoon in a continuous ribbon. Leave the batter to rest for 15 minutes.

In the meantime, heat the oil in a large skillet or saucepan over medium-high heat. Dip each piece of banana into the batter and ensure it is coated completely. Add the banana pieces to the oil and fry them for 1 to 2 minutes, or until they are golden brown, rotating them every 30 seconds to achieve even browning.

Transfer the bananas to paper towels to drain. Serve the bananas warm.

TIPS: These banana fritters are superb with ice cream!

You can also fry other ingredients, like sweet potato slices, taro and jackfruit, using this recipe as a guide.

PANDAN CREPES WITH SWEET COCONUT AND PEANUT FILLING

(KUIH DADAR)

This is one of my favorite sweet snacks ever! When visiting family in Malaysia, we used to get plastic clamshell boxes filled with different sticky sweets, like an assorted chocolate box but better. Most of them were glutinous rice–based or rice flour dumplings, all bright and colorful. I always grabbed the *kuih dadar* first! The soft, pillowy crepe has a beautiful warm aroma of pandan. It's like a mix of vanilla and coconut. The filling is sweet, jammy, chewy coconut. I've included toasted peanuts for a textural contrast. The savory crunch is delectable.

MAKES 6 TO 7 PANCAKES

CREPE BATTER

1 cup (120 g) all-purpose flour

1 large egg

1¼ cups (300 ml) full-fat coconut milk

¼ tsp salt

2 tbsp (30 ml) pandan extract

4 to 6 drops green food coloring

Unsalted butter or rice bran, canola or grapeseed oil, as needed

FILLING

7½ tbsp (90 g) palm sugar, finely shaved or grated

⅓ cup (80 ml) water

¾ cup (68 g) toasted desiccated coconut, soaked in 3 tbsp (45 ml) water for 10 minutes

2 tbsp (30 ml) full-fat coconut cream

2 tbsp (16 g) finely ground toasted, salted peanuts

To make the crepe batter, whisk together the flour, egg, coconut milk, salt and pandan extract in a large bowl until the ingredients are smooth. Add the food coloring, whisking between every 1 or 2 drops, until the batter turns a bright, grassy green. Set the batter aside to rest while you make the filling.

To make the filling, combine the palm sugar and water in a medium skillet over medium heat. Stir continuously for approximately 5 minutes, until the sugar is dissolved and comes to a simmer. Add the desiccated coconut and stir well to combine. Add the coconut cream and stir to combine. Turn off the heat and mix in the peanuts. Mix well and leave the filling to cool to room temperature.

Place a medium non-stick skillet over a low heat. Grease the skillet with a dab of butter. Pour in approximately ¼ cup (60 ml) of the batter into the skillet while swirling it around to form a very thin layer of batter that covers the entire bottom of the skillet. Cook the crepe for 2 to 3 minutes on each side, or until the cooked surface appears opaque and dry to the touch but has not browned at all and the upward-facing surface has become dry to the touch. Transfer the crepe to a plate and cover it with a clean tea towel while you repeat the preceding steps with the remaining batter, greasing the skillet between each crepe.

Once all the crepes have been made, place 1½ to 2 tablespoons (23 to 30 g) of the filling on the bottom third of each crepe. Fold the sides of the crepe inward and then roll the crepe up like a spring roll. Slice it in half to serve.

TIP: These crepes are best eaten the day they are made. The filling can be made ahead. Simply reheat the filling in a medium skillet over medium heat with 2 tablespoons (30 ml) full-fat coconut milk.

MALAYSIAN SWEET POTATO DOUGHNUTS
(KUIH KERIA)

Malaysians are extremely innovative when it comes to creating sweet treats out of ordinary ingredients. Pineapples, coconut, glutinous rice, sweet potatoes and dried beans are some of the more iconic ingredients in Malaysian desserts. *Kuih keria*, or sweet potato doughnuts, are one of the most loved and simplest treats to make. They're vegan too! These pillowy doughnuts are frosted in a crispy white shell of sugar that cracks and crumbles when you bite through it. These doughnuts are divine when washed down with a creamy coffee or hot chocolate. I loved these after-school treats made by my aunts when I was young. I used to nibble off all the sugar coating first before digging into the still-warm, fluffy, doughy center.

MAKES 12 SMALL DOUGHNUT BALLS OR 8 SMALL RING DOUGHNUTS

1 cup (160 g) peeled and finely chopped sweet potato

¼ tsp salt

½ tsp baking powder

½ cup (60 g) all-purpose flour, plus more as needed

Rice bran, canola or grapeseed oil, as needed

1 cup plus 2 tsp (200 g) sugar

6 tbsp (90 ml) water

Bring a medium pot of water to a boil over high heat. Add the sweet potato and boil it for 10 to 15 minutes, until it is completely tender. Drain the sweet potato and, while it is still hot, mash it until it is smooth and pasty. Add the salt and baking powder and mix thoroughly. Leave the sweet potato mixture to cool for 15 to 20 minutes.

Add the flour to the potato mixture and combine the ingredients well. Knead the mixture for 5 to 6 minutes, until a soft, smooth dough is formed. The dough should hold together on its own and should not stick to your hand. If you find the mixture is too wet, add ½ tablespoon (4 g) of flour and continue kneading. Allow the dough to rest for 5 to 10 minutes before forming it into 12 small balls or 8 small ring doughnuts.

Fill a large saucepan or deep skillet over medium heat with 2 inches (5 cm) of oil. Heat the oil to 350°F (177°C).

Working in batches so as not to overcrowd the saucepan, carefully slide the doughnuts into the oil. Fry the doughnuts for 6 to 8 minutes total, rotating them frequently, until all of their sides are golden brown. Transfer the doughnuts to paper towels to drain.

While the doughnuts drain, place a large dry skillet over medium heat. Add the sugar and water and stir until the sugar completely dissolves and a syrup is formed. Allow the syrup to come up to a boil and then reduce the heat to medium-low. Simmer the syrup for 3 to 4 minutes. To check if the sugar crust is ready, use a spatula to pick some of the syrup up and let it fall from a height back into the skillet. If it appears thickened and tends to fall in heavy clumps, the syrup is ready. Turn off the heat and then add the doughnuts to the syrup. Toss the doughnuts with the spatula to completely coat them. Keep tossing the doughnuts in the syrup for 1 to 2 minutes, until the syrup begins to crystallize into a crispy white shell.

Once the doughnuts have formed a shell and there's no liquid in the skillet, the doughnuts can be transferred to a wire rack or tray to cool for 5 to 10 minutes before serving.

These doughnuts can be kept in an airtight container in a cool place (not in the refrigerator) for 2 to 3 days.

THAI STICKY RICE AND MANGO

This dessert is so simple, yet it's one of the most pleasing sweets I've ever eaten. On a warm night in Bangkok, Thailand, one of my best friends and I sat on rickety plastic chairs in a busy night market and tucked into the sweet mango and the savory, oily sticky rice. It was a carefree, happy moment captured perfectly by this dessert.

SERVES 6

2 cups (420 g) Thai glutinous rice, rinsed until the water runs clear and soaked for at least 1 hour

1⅔ cups plus ¼ cup (460 ml) full-fat coconut milk, divided

5 tbsp plus 2 tsp (68 g) sugar, divided

½ tsp salt

2 tbsp (30 ml) rice bran, canola or grapeseed oil

3 oz (84 g) dried split yellow mung beans, soaked for at least 1 hour in warm water

3 medium ripe mangoes

In a steamer, steam the glutinous rice for 15 to 20 minutes, or until the grains are completely cooked through. Transfer the cooked rice to a medium bowl.

In the meantime, combine 1⅓ cups (320 ml) of the coconut milk, 5 tablespoons (60 g) of the sugar and the salt in a small saucepan over medium heat, stirring until the sugar and salt have fully dissolved. Once the coconut milk comes to a simmer, remove the saucepan from the heat.

Slowly stir the reserved ¼ cup (60 ml) of the coconut milk into the rice until all the milk is fully incorporated into the rice. Cover the rice with plastic wrap to prevent it from drying out, and then set it aside.

In a small saucepan over medium heat, stir together the remaining ⅓ cup (80 ml) of coconut milk and 2 teaspoons (8 g) of sugar until the sugar has completely dissolved. Once the coconut milk comes to a simmer, remove the saucepan from the heat and set it aside to cool to room temperature.

Heat the oil in a small clean skillet over medium heat. Drain the mung beans very well. Add them to the oil and fry them for 4 to 5 minutes, or until they have deepened in color and become crispy, stirring frequently. Remove the mung beans from the heat and transfer them to paper towels to cool to room temperature.

Peel the mangoes, and slice the cheeks off. Cut each cheek into thin slices.

Divide the sticky rice among 6 individual plates and top each portion with a sliced mango cheek, a drizzle of the sweetened coconut milk and a sprinkle of the crispy mung beans.

MALAYSIAN SWEET AND SAVORY PANCAKE TURNOVERS

(APAM BALIK)

It may be strange to think of creamed corn in a dessert, but it is one of my favorite things about these deliciously fluffy pancakes. The creamy corn, caramelly brown sugar and savory peanuts work fantastically together when they are nestled in the center of a warm, soft and airy pancake with toasted edges. These pancakes typically come in two different forms from Malaysian street food carts: thick and thin. The thin versions are wafer-like, crisp pancakes and tend to be a little drier. This version is the thick, cakey version. It is filling and buttery. You can configure the filling of each pancake to your preference. As a kid, I'd pile on the corn and peanuts until the pancakes were almost too difficult to fold over. Get creative with the fillings: chocolate, nuts, bananas, jams, peanut butter, cheese or anything else you love!

MAKES 5 PANCAKE TURNOVERS

1 cup (120 g) all-purpose flour

½ cup (60 g) self-rising flour

2 tbsp (24 g) granulated sugar

¾ tsp baking soda

1½ tsp (5 g) instant yeast

2 tsp (10 ml) pure vanilla extract

1 large egg

1 cup (240 ml) warm milk

¼ tsp salt

Rice bran, canola or grapeseed oil, as needed

2½ tbsp (35 g) salted butter, divided into 5 portions

1 (14-oz [392-g]) can creamed corn, divided into 5 portions

5 tbsp (40 g) finely chopped toasted, salted peanuts, divided into 5 portions

5 tbsp (45 g) brown sugar, divided into 5 portions

In a large bowl, whisk together the all-purpose flour, self-rising flour, granulated sugar, baking soda, yeast, vanilla, egg, milk and salt. Whisk until the ingredients are completely smooth and incorporated. Cover the bowl tightly with plastic wrap and let the batter rest in a warm place for at least 45 minutes, or until it has doubled in volume.

Heat an 8-inch (20-cm) nonstick skillet over low heat. Brush the bottom and sides of the skillet with the oil. Ladle ¾ cup (180 ml) of the batter into the skillet. Use the base of the ladle to spread the batter evenly around the bottom of the skillet. (Tilting and swirling the skillet will help spread the batter out.) Cook the batter, undisturbed, for 4 to 5 minutes. Bubbles should form on the surface of the pancake and the surface should be mostly dry, with some tacky areas.

Spread 1 portion butter, 1 portion of the creamed corn, 1 portion of the peanuts and 1 portion of the brown sugar onto one half of the pancake's surface. Then, using a spatula, carefully fold over the other half of the pancake, forming a sandwich-like shape. Gently press down on the turnover a few times and cook the turnover for 1 to 2 minutes, until the corn, butter and sugar form a cohesive filling.

Remove the turnover from the skillet. Repeat this process with the remaining batter and filling components.

Wrap the turnovers in parchment paper or transfer them to a paper bag to eat as a snack on the go, or slice the turnovers in half and serve them with ice cream.

Thank you to Ben Cole for your warmth, generosity and keen eye. You have created stunning photography in this book. I have loved working with you.

Thank you to Cecilia Bloom—your food-styling talent, humor and spirit were key ingredients in creating this special book. I have loved working with you also.

Special thanks to Jenna Fagan, Meg Baskis and the team at Page Street Publishing. Your support, guidance and positivity has made this a fantastic experience.

Thank you to my family. Your constant support, happiness, encouragement and pursuit of deliciousness fill my heart with joy.

Thank you to my dearest friends, who embrace these adventures with me. Your positive words lift me when I need it most.

Thank you to all those who have supported me through *MasterChef Australia* and beyond. Your support means the world to me. Whether you are connected with me on social media, you have purchased this book, you have attended one of my events or pop-ups or you have supported me from afar, I hope that I have helped make your lives a little more delicious.

A lawyer by trade, Sarah Tiong has always had an undeniable and unstoppable passion for food. Her travels to Southeast Asia over the past twenty years have inspired her passion for creating community and connection through food. Cooking and feeding others encompass everything Sarah treasures about culture, history and sharing knowledge.

In 2017, Sarah competed on *MasterChef Australia* and earned her place within the top-six finalists. Establishing herself as a strong cook from the get-go, Sarah became a viewer favorite with her ability to showcase her unique and masterful skills in Southeast Asian cuisine.

After competing on *MasterChef Australia*, Sarah's world completely changed. She created her own pop-up hawker stall called Pork Party in Sydney, specializing in Asian-inspired pork dishes. Sarah also works with leading food and hospitality brands to develop recipes and cooks at demonstrations and pop-up dining experiences. Her enthusiasm and experience has led to features in magazines and podcasts such as J-Style, Departure Lounge and *Better Homes and Gardens*; appearances on the Australian TV show *Studio 10*; a position as a key speaker with the Japan National Tourism Organization; multiple brand endorsements and even a role as a judge for the Australian BBQ Wars.

Sarah returned to *MasterChef Australia* as a contestant in series 12 in 2020. Sarah also continues to run Pork Party and work as a private chef and recipe developer.

CONNECT WITH SARAH ON SOCIAL MEDIA:

Website: sarahtiong.com

Instagram: @fillmytummy

Facebook: /SarahTiongAU

YouTube: /sarahtiong

INDEX